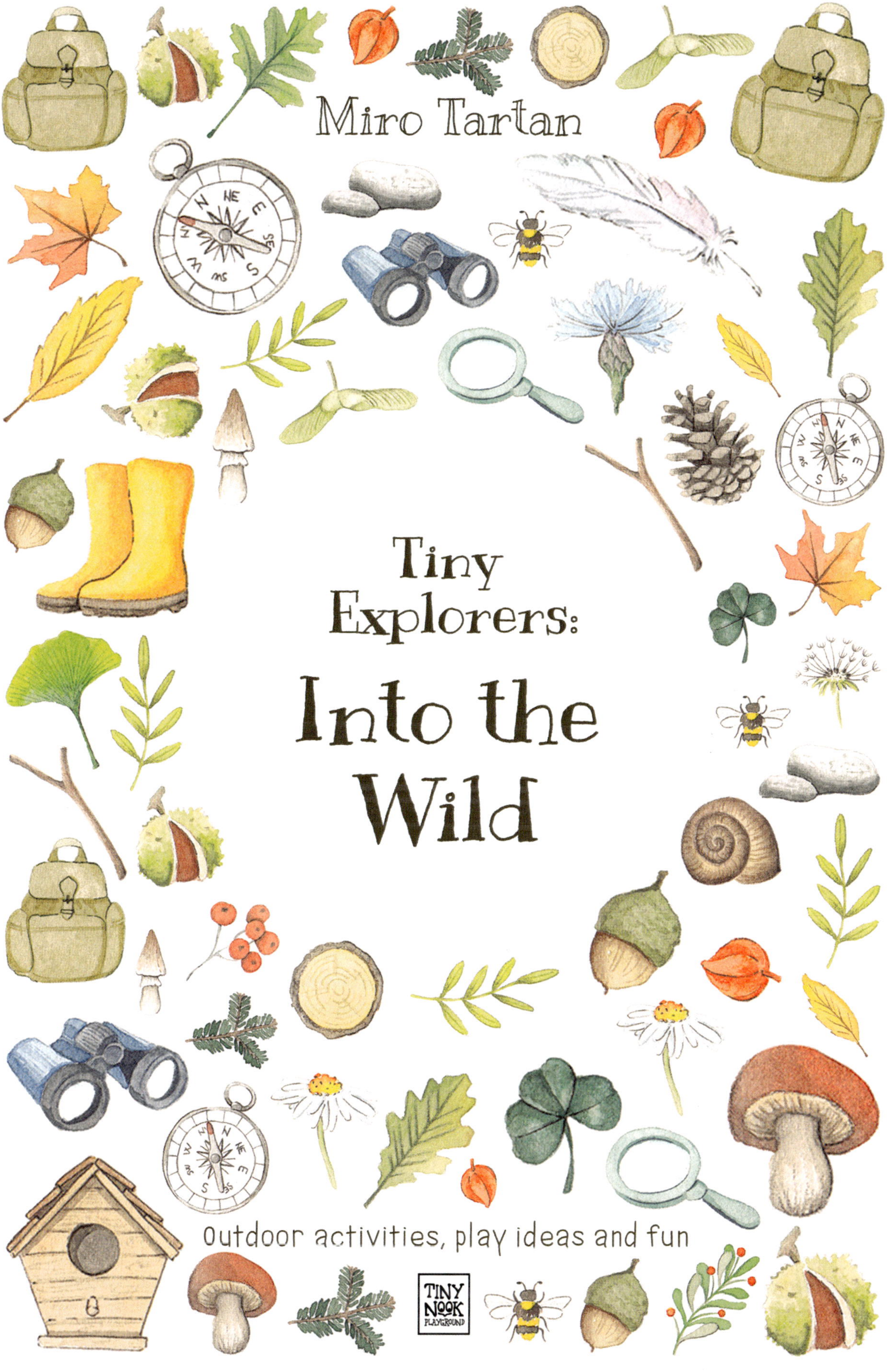

Miro Tartan

Tiny Explorers: Into the Wild

Outdoor activities, play ideas and fun

TINY NOOK PLAYGROUND

Dedication

For my tiny explorers A & G, never lose your enthusiasm!

For my beloved better half who has supported this project in every possible way, couldn't have written this book without you!

Text, illustrations, photographs and design by Miro Tartan
Edited by Laura Bingham

ISBN 978-1-913691-05-9

Introduction

DISCONNECT, OPEN THE DOOR, RECONNECT

A long time ago, humans had a special relationship with nature. Mother Nature provided humans with food and everything necessary for living. But then humanity evolved and, somewhere along the way, humans wanted independence. They started building human-made environments. Maybe humans got scared of the rain, wind and sun, so they secluded themselves – first in caves and afterwards between walls. This meant they were protected from the weather but it also meant that humans missed nature. They would try to recreate it indoors – with flowery curtains and paintings of forests and birds. It wasn't the same as being outdoors and directly involved in nature though.

Now humans have evolved so much that they rarely spend time in nature because they have too many other things to do. The good news is that nature is still there, here, all around us – loving, kind, eventful, mysterious, patient, cheerful. It's easy to rebuild a connection with nature. People just have to disconnect, breathe in, breathe out, get dressed, open the door, step out, reconnect. Having a strong connection with nature can help us find much-needed balance in life; from physical to mental health, for the young, the old and everyone in-between. Want to get the most out of this relationship? Why not start early? Why not show your children the joys of nature whilst they're little?

By taking our children outside, we can help build their relationship with nature and this will benefit them hugely. Playing outside is an engaging, inspiring and creative way to help children understand the way the world works. From observing the cycle of life to experimenting with physical forces, nature is both an educational space and a good teacher. Introducing outdoor play supports our little ones into becoming focused, self-confident individuals with positive thoughts, optimistic behaviours and a healthy imagination.

I'd love to say 'I spent all my childhood outdoors playing with sticks and rocks, went back home only at sunset, oh and the rain... who cared about the rain!' But truth be told, as an introverted child born in an urban area, without a garden, I spent most of my early childhood days indoors, building blanket forts under the kitchen table, hugging my teddies, eating far more than 5-a-day plastic fruits and drinking tons of imaginary tea.

I must have been taken on various nature walks when I was little, but the first real memory I have relating to nature is pretty late (around 7 years old) when we went camping. This was the start of a very special relationship with nature. Ah, the smell of the forest after the rain, the taste of clear spring water, the walk in the woods where we began singing our hearts out on our way back just because we could, the sweet feeling of going to bed after a full day outdoors – with numb feet and cold noses! I had to spend a week without my precious toys, but tell you what, seems that my teddies survived without their daily hugs and I, not only 'survived', but thrived and found a friend for life, nature.

Whilst on that very first camping trip, I found the most magnificent hiking stick ever. I believed it was magical because one of the ends resembled a deer's head with majestic antlers. I loved that stick and took it back to our tent with me. After a while, one of the antlers broke so I had to find a way to fix it. How do you fix a stick in the wilderness? I learned it the hard way – that pine sap makes great glue, not just for a broken stick but for fingers as well. It glued the stick and stuck my fingers! But hey, at least it got fixed and it had such a wonderful unmistakable smell.

There are lots of special memories I have which involve nature. One of these was when I was camping with my dad a few years after that first camping holiday. 'Miro, quick! Come look, I've found something!' I hurried over to where my dad was peering by a rock. 'I think I've found the King of Beetles', he said, showing me the most magnificent creatures I had ever seen – stag beetles. I must have missed caring for my teddies a lot because I remember starting to look for injured beetles, building them cardboard dens, giving them food and releasing them after a thorough inspection – even kings need to be cared for, right?

I also learnt to cook the most amazing mushroom stew after a day of hiking. From a handful of foraged chanterelles and probably a bag of onions just to make sure it was enough for everyone, my dad showed me how to make it. I still cook it to this day. Thank you, Dad!

For me, the outdoor experiences helped me develop certain crafting skills as I found myself in a world of basic elements but still wanted to replicate activities and objects found in everyday life. Imagine how proud I was when I built my very own puppet – my first project with using a whittling knife (with very cautious supervision), a piece of wood and somo pins. Creating offered limitless satisfaction and opened a world of ideas that kept my mind busy even on my way back to the city.

Looking back now, I wonder what my childhood would have been like if I had been introduced to nature from an earlier age – lying on the grass as a baby looking up at the clouds, learning to toddle in the mud, holding a worm in my chubby toddler hands. It's never too early for a child to explore the outside world.

A NOTE FOR PARENTS

As parents, we play a big role in all aspects of our child's development, and it can be daunting. But introducing your children to nature doesn't have to feel overwhelming or like another 'job' to have to try and find time for. Within this book, I will show you ways in which you can introduce your child to a whole world of experiences with nature. The activities vary in complexity and are clearly labelled for you to see which activity is appropriate for your circumstance. By using this book, you will guide your child on a journey into discovering nature.

I find that my two boys are always happier (and calmer) after we have spent time being 'wild'. They are two very different personalities and it is always a challenge to find ways to keep them both entertained, I think all parents have this worry at one time or another. Being young is difficult for them – they are trying to build relationships with each other while coping with sometimes unknown emotions. When we are outside they forget about their toys and rivalries and focus on gathering, building, creating. I hope this book helps you and your family in a similar way, providing you with many hours of fun time and eventually, great memories.

I believe the more time you spend in nature with your children, the easier it is to find ways to engage with them in all areas of life. Spending time in nature, once you find different ways to do so, doesn't feel like a chore. With my little ones, I know that every minute in nature is a minute I am doing the right thing for them.

From simple things like deciding to walk to school one day rather than take the car, to taking the family camping or engaging in outdoor activities, we can facilitate building bridges in two directions, between them and nature but also between them and us.

Don't worry, you don't have to take your child camping for them to get their first experience with nature. There are many ways we engage with nature without it being a full-on camping trip... we have pots of flowers, we can visit friends with gardens, go to parks, admire the trees on our way back from nursery or school. Each activity outside is more import ant than the time spent in front of a TV or tablet. It creates skills that our children can develop and use when they are older. It will also help equip them with tools that will help them understand their surroundings and the wider world. Spending time outside helps children to develop into mindful, caring, independent, eyes-wide-open-feet-on-the-ground adults.

With a bit of attentiveness, awareness and mindfulness, we can help enhance some of the most mundane, everyday activities into experiences for our kids. For example, next time you take a walk in the park, watch out, look around, you never know when you may find a magical item. It could be the roundest rock, the most colourful leaf, or maybe a magical stick with a deer-shaped end – you'll know when you've found it! Your little one will be excited and, next thing you know, they'll be on a hunt of their own for all these treasures.

Remember to take a moment to talk about one of these walks, activities or adventures at the end of the day. Use this time to connect. Find out what the little ones liked most. Ask them how they felt, what they thought. Was there something new they hadn't seen before? Did they learn something? Do they want to tell someone else in the family about it? Share with them what you liked and how much you appreciate their attentiveness, patience or bravery. Your child might even surprise you with coming up with a new idea for an activity to enjoy in the future. Taking time to share your experiences with your child can really enhance your relationship and help them to develop emotionally.

THIS PROJECT: A STORY

Once upon a time, in a little English town in an area surrounded by green hills, magical air, lively lakes and vivid wildlife, there was a mummy, a daddy and two little princes who had just moved from a land of high steel buildings and long big roads full of metal self-propelled carriages. Mummy and Daddy weren't quite the definitions of Homo Outdoorsyus but the surrounding lakes and the magical forests put a spell on them... well, mostly on Mummy. Since then, the two little princes were really energetic and thirsty for knowledge. Mummy started to use the magic in the air and found... basically ways to keep the little princes busy.

In all truthfulness, I feel that this environment is what I needed to help me feel alive and unleash my creativity. My creative gene finds its roots at least two generations back on my maternal line, but even the most creative mind needs a muse. In my case, it was nature. Apart from a few camping trips as a child, I had an urban life. It was wonderful to be back with nature again when my two children came along and we decided to move to a more rural scenery.

I often found myself playing outside with my boys and began trying to think of new ways to entertain them outside of the house. I started by searching on the Internet for activities and then adapted them based on my own children's interests. We all got engaged and after a while, we have started making some of our own original nature-based activities.

Because of my love for drawing and painting, I began sketching along throughout the day with a diary-like religiousness. Representing our activities, both adapted and original, on paper was fun and the kids loved it as it enabled us to discuss them at bedtime. Soon enough, my sketches from a small handmade notebook started looking very much like a mini nature journal. I shared a few pages on social media and, because they became popular, I decided to share the notebook as a free online e-book.

I have had lots of messages, shares and positive feedback which I am very humbled and grateful for. The support encouraged me to create this; a very special project which I hope will enable you to start your own nature diary. Creating this book has been a project of passion with many late nights working, but the support from people on social media has inspired me to keep going.

HOW TO MAKE NATURE MORE APPEALING TO CHILDREN

I'll start by stating something obvious and well known: Children learn by the power of example. They absorb both knowledge and feelings with an efficiency that we wish we have as grown-ups. A child's way of thinking and personality is shaped by whatever happens around them and to them.

We all have good habits and bad habits. Whether we like it or not, as you already know by now, little ones start to copy some of our habits – for example, if they see us enjoying a good book, they are more likely to have an interest in reading too. The same goes for nature – having a good habit of going out on walks, increases the chances of the child becoming a nature enthusiast as they grow up. It's not a habit yet? Well, we can try and work on it, right? I assure you, the benefits of spending time outside are plenty. Already do it or want to do it but don't know how to make it more interesting? Now, that's a good start. This book will help you on that journey.

How do we bring our little ones closer to nature? It starts with you. You have to be the initiator and set the example. For a while, anyway, because as soon as it becomes a habit, they will be the ones saying, 'Let's take a walk', as it becomes familiar, fun and even gives them comfort. Again, if you already do it, good job! You don't? You are not alone. But you might need to 'fake it till you make it' just to help encourage your child to go out. Once you're outside, it all becomes easier.

It can be very simple to engage your child with nature. When outdoors, show them a dandelion clock and blow it together. After enjoying the fragrance of different flowers, ask them to close their eyes and recognise them by scent alone. Touch and feel the textures of plants (careful of stingy ones). Find minibeasts, let them hear the sounds of nature; chirping birds, falling rain, leaves rustling under tiny feet, the wind. Have picnics in the woods (but not on teddy bears' picnic day!), build tents and forts in the garden (I'll show you one later, but there are many ideas out there). Read outside, sing outside, play their favourite indoor game – you guessed it – outside! Find ways to combine their interests with nature. Get those cars, dinosaurs, unicorns and dolls outside (those that are mud-proof, otherwise there might be some drama).

Do they love cars? Help them build a big motorway from twigs, add ramps and tunnels from bark and leaves. Dinosaurs? Make a dinosaur birthday party in a muddy puddle. Splish! Splash! Unicorns? Create a fairy garden riding school for the braver fairies.

If muddiness becomes an issue, well... cleaning afterwards is a learning activity too. Play with everything you find, talk about everything you see, document it all with pictures, and, I can't repeat myself enough, have FUN!

BOREDOM? WHAT ABOUT IT?

Let's say it's springtime, nature flourishes, you are having fun outside but after a few weeks, it all starts to become a little dull. If you are afraid boredom might find its way into your newly established outside fun routine, you have the right to think so. It probably will. That's normal, but don't worry, there are many ways to prevent boredom from setting in.

Fight boredom by inventing games and stories around the activities or trips. Encourage the little ones to invent some as well. Even better, embrace boredom! Bored people come up with some of the greatest ideas. Their minds just need a spark to start the fireworks even in the dullest of moments.

Last autumn, we were taking a walk home from preschool. It was a well-known path, not the greatest of weather, and none of us were particularly energetic or enthusiastic about the walk. A (my eldest child) observed the colour-changing trees and started to be fascinated by the fact that some of the leaves were changing to red. He picked up a fallen red leaf in his hand and walked with it for a while, continuing to look at it with interest. Then, he started looking like someone who just had the best idea ever. He found a green one too and was the proud owner of two signals. With a big smile on his face, he instructed everyone (meaning myself and his little brother – G) that whenever the 'red signal was on' we must stop until the 'green signal'. He held up the green leaf and we walked. He held up the red leaf and we stopped. He found this great fun. Whilst we were walking along playing the game, I then had the idea to add something extra – every time the red signal was held up and we had to stop, G and I would look for something interesting around us – an object, a smell, a sound. It was a brilliantly creative game which had been thought up during what we thought was a dull walk!

If you know that one of your children may not find the upcoming nature trail interesting, then be prepared! Make preparations the way you would for an important expedition. Location. Transport. Itinerary. Expected encounters. This will help to create intrigue, excitement and enthusiasm, so much so that they will find the nature walk interesting after all!

Draw a rough map of the area you are visiting or find a place that already has a map of the surroundings. Trace a route and mark the spots of interest – set milestones. These preparations have the potential of making your child be more space and time-aware. It builds up a sense of eagerness towards the trip as well as a great sense of accomplishment at the end of it.

BRING NATURE INSIDE

I think the love for nature is in our DNA but we need to both activate it and nourish it. Going outside is certainly a good way, and often the most obvious way, to do this – as it's away from the many distractions of the home with all its gadgets. But you can go beyond just exploring nature outside, you can also bring nature inside. No really! I'm not suggesting this for the sake of bad weather days – as even bad weather days can provide us with endless outdoor fun (splashing in puddles, feeling snow falling on our tongues, letting the wind whip our hair across our faces...). Spending time outside during bad weather is a great way to expand your child's love of nature and also help to lift their spirits. So, why am I suggesting bringing nature inside? This is because nature doesn't need to solely be enjoyed outside, children can benefit from connecting with nature indoors too and it can further fuel their activities.

You could make a nature corner in your house. We have one in the conservatory, so everything can be at hand when we go out to explore: wellies and rainy day outfit, a foraging container, a backpack filled with a magnifying glass, binoculars (tissue rolls taped together work just fine for smaller kids), compass, maps, our favourite nature guide, our beloved bug viewer jar, duck food...

Within our nature corner, we also have a 'nature table' and change the themes every now and then. This week is going to be about birds (feathers, books, twigs for nests, etc.), next week will be about trees, and then flowers, and then rocks and soil, and then... I think you get the picture! We find a nature-related theme and then start searching for related material, we bring it inside and have discussions around it. I encourage you to find books (maybe from the library) that are appropriate for the theme, flashcards or posters for reference can be good too. Have a basket full of little treasures found on your walks and use them as teaching or craft material.

Fill in a bookcase display with nature-themed books (what a good place for this one, too) next to the one with your favourite storybooks and infuse a little bit of nature-loving joy to that cosy reading nook where the stories can be shared and enjoyed. Display nature-related art on walls, maybe made by you (you'll find plenty of materials in this book) and small pots of indoor plants that children can take care of.

And to get to the more hands-on part, make a nature journal that can keep you busy for a good amount of time. Don't know where to start? No worries, you can start with the nature journal that I've made (a companion for this book), but the main idea is to collect memories, materials and items from your walks, make sketches of what you saw or where you were, write in the time and the weather, the place that you visited, draw a small map and involve the little ones as much as possible.

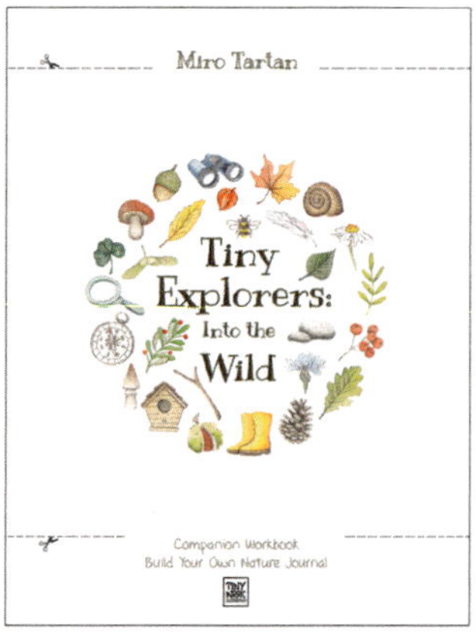

THE ACTIVITIES: ENGAGE, APPRECIATE, HAVE FUN

The activities included in this book are fun for all. I do not make age recommendations for each of the proposed activities because, regardless of age, little ones will be really proud of their achievements and you will as well. For us, both G (2) and A (4) show interest and engage fully in the activities. They don't always care about the end result but are more interested in the process of creating something. Of course, a 2-year-old will not always be able to do everything by himself, but G was willing to at least have a go with most of the activities, and there were always moments when I needed to step in to help too. Would I restrict these activities to under 7s or under 12s? Certainly not. Many of these tasks are even fun for grown-ups! Enjoying and being creative with nature has no boundaries when it comes to age.

What I would like to recommend though is being extra cautious. You will know your own child's capabilities, but there are a few things to keep in mind. First, I can't stress enough how important it is for your child to be over the 'I sense the world through my mouth' phase as many of the items are small and there is a high risk of choking. Secondly, make sure your children don't have a tree nut allergy if you are going to use them in the activities.

Also, some plants or berries might not be suitable for use. Natural doesn't automatically mean safe. Be sure that what you are touching is not poisonous – if you aren't sure, then err on the side of caution. If a plant looks new to you, leave it, find something more common. Although most mushrooms are safe to touch, you can make a no-touching rule for smaller children, just to be sure. There are plenty of apps that can even recognise plants by image. We are living in an age of advanced technology so make the most of it.

Another safety tip, watch your children constantly when they are using tools that might harm them. Children of any age like being in charge and this makes them confident in their abilities. Let them try but offer to help if you feel they might need it, or keep them involved by asking them to help you when doing the important stuff (G felt very important when I asked him to hold my hand while making a drill hole into a piece of bark). Last but not least in this list of safety-related points is that you'll have to take care as well. By practising being careful yourself, children will learn to be aware of the constant need for being safe – remember what I said earlier about children learning through watching how we behave?

Make sure your tiny explorers (and yourself) are well-rested before starting an activity. At times, as with any high focus, energy-consuming task, one might get to a point where it feels frustrating. For this reason, I have included in all activities some special, easy to read indicators which show you how much concentration and time a task can take. Each task has a key which shows messiness, time, effort and theme. If you feel like it's not the best time for messy play – pick another one. If there isn't much time to carry out an activity pick a less time-consuming one. With rested minds and buckets full of patience and motivation, you are all set.

And remember, the time spent together while doing the activity is more important than the actual result.

The activities are grouped into five different themes and you don't have to work through them in any particular order. You choose which activity suits you on that particular day.

FIRST STEPS INTO NATURE: This theme is about catching the child's attention with some introduction to nature activities. Some of these activities can also be used within other activities too – you may make something on one task which then comes in useful for another task. Reusing items is very important for our environment. Most of these activities use ordinary objects found in nature in creative ways which help to stimulate a child's imagination and encourage a bit of outside-the-box thinking. You may be an avid outdoor fan and love interacting with nature, but even these introductory tasks for your children will have you involved, learning and enjoying the fun too.

PLAY PRETEND: What a senseless, soulless world it would be without stories! There are theories that say humans' capacity for telling stories was a greater revolution than the farming one because imagination facilitated exponential brain development. For each activity, I've set up the narrative but feel free to come up with something even more appealing to your little ones. Your tiny explorer will communicate in their own way. Pretend play helps children to develop social and emotional skills and, whilst coupled with these tasks, they will improve their dexterity too.

GET CLOSER TO WILDLIFE: Take your green, commando-like uniforms, cover yourselves with branches, 'face paint' yourselves with mud. Find a hideout, keep your binoculars close, get some tea and plan to stay for hours without making too much noise. This is real, we are getting close to wildlife. Track every move in your explorer's journal, draw every creature in detail, take photos and record priceless videos. Nah, I'm kidding, doesn't have to be this real... unless you want to!

MAKE SOME ART: It's really important for explorers to be artists at heart. To be honest, it's important for all of us to be artists. Representing what we see, expressing our feelings and excitement through various kinds of art is a form of relaxation, a way to communicate and, at times of need, even a way of healing. This theme contains art-oriented activities to do in between the 'exploring expeditions'. Our little explorers need tools to cope with the everyday complexity of their development and the best way to relax that left (logical) side of the brain is by exercising the right (artsy) one. Using the right hemisphere of the brain, and helping to expand its potential, is as important for our well-being as physical exercise.

LEARN THROUGH PLAY: All of the other activities are full of educational hooks that can be expanded upon, but the ones in this theme specifically focus on the ability to learn through play. The subjects in this group include sun and light, the flow of time and the circle of life. These are all approached in ways that involve a natural element whilst being educational with a playful twist.

Some of the activities involve set-up time. Your tiny explorers can help you prepare for the activity – they'll enjoy passing you the things you need. If they are engaged and involved during the set-up process, imagine the interest while performing the activity itself! You can show the activity to your child in advance, have them look at the various steps that the task involves. You could even write the step numbers on a piece of paper and tick them off when you complete them. I know my little ones get excited when they tick items off lists.

Each activity has a 'Development' section which helps you understand what areas or phases of child development the respective activity supports. These tasks are not just about enjoying nature and having fun, but also a great way to help your child through various developmental stages such as dexterity, fine motor skills, concentration, and much more, depending on the type of activity.

I hope the activities in this book will be a source of inspiration for you. Let your imagination and crafty spirit fly and enjoy trying the different activities. You can tweak the tasks to make them relevant to you or you could skip to the 'Take it Further' and 'Other ideas' sections as they are loaded with many more hours of nature fun.

Fun facts and tips can be found throughout the book too. These can fuel conversations around the activity but also inspire you to create other activities.

Remember, whatever the outcome of the activity and its finished result, children have already won a great deal by spending time with you. They learn by example and seeing you engaged, resilient and patient is a wonderful gift to give them.

Appreciate this time spent together and the memories that you are making (take tons of pictures), but most of all don't forget to have fun! Share the super fun moments and completed activities with the Tiny Explorers community by tagging them with #TinyExplorersIntoTheWild #TinyNookPlayground.

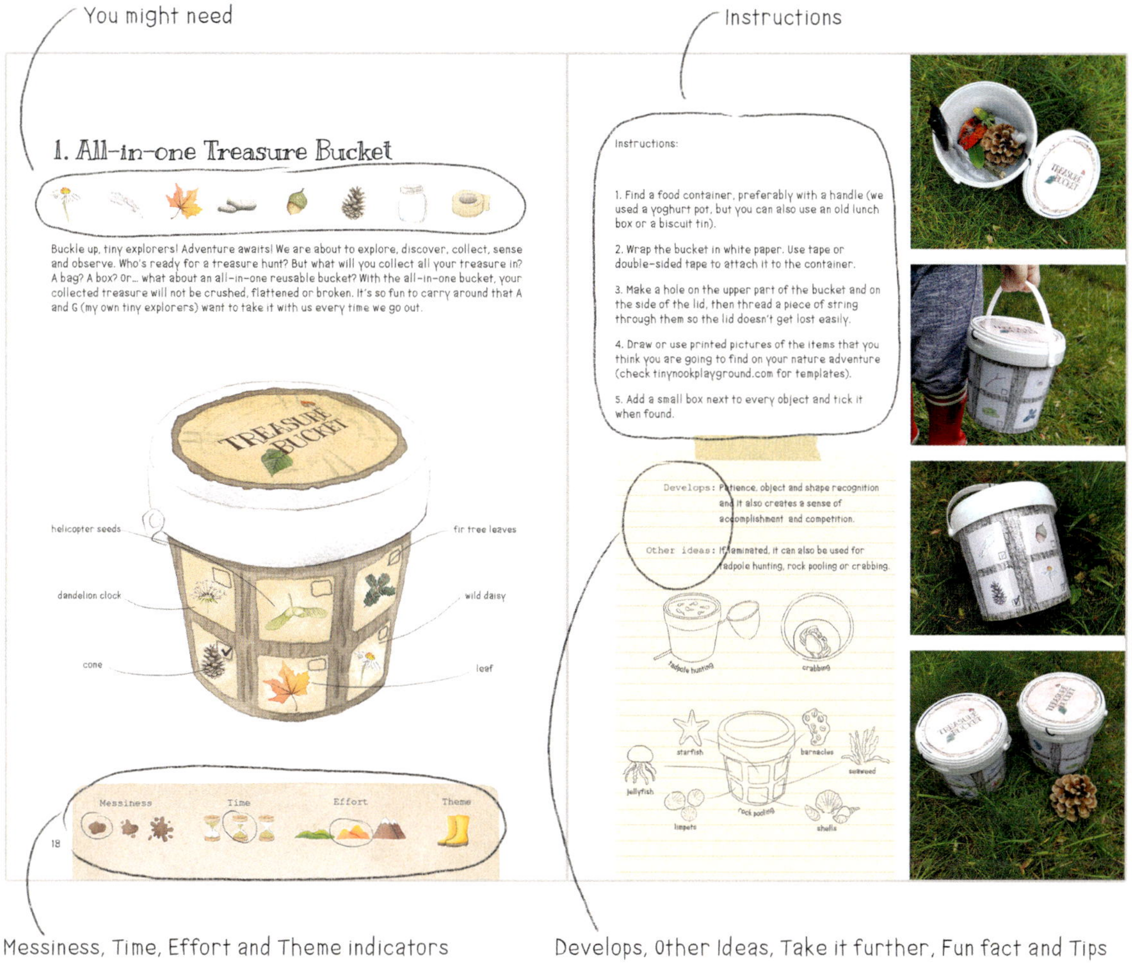

You might need

Nature

plants

snail shells

leaves

acorns

cones

rocks

flowers

moss

twigs

petals

chestnuts

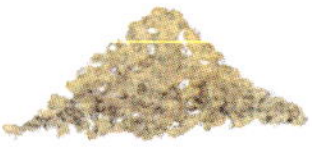
bird seeds

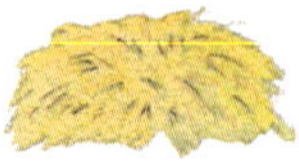
straw

feathers

bark

sand

soil

waste

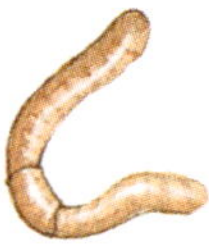
worms

Tools

knife

scissors

drill

nuts and bolts

rolling pin

Crafts

card or paper

paint

markers

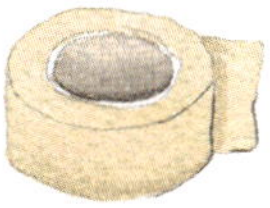
double-sided tape

cardboard

sun print paper

fabric

clay

contact paper

food colouring

string

glue

Other

sun

water

plastic container

spray bottle

kitchenware

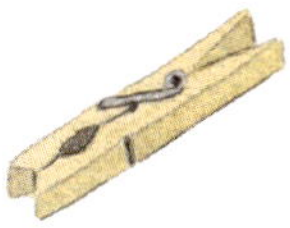
clothespins

egg box

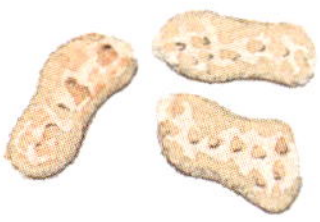
peanuts

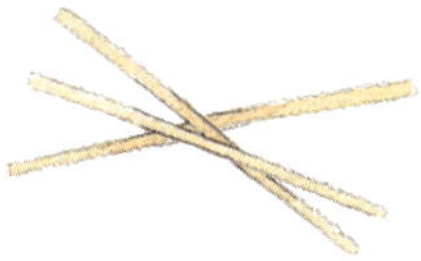
skewers

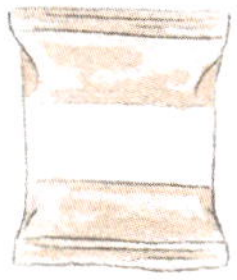
gelatin

plywood

wooden frame

1. All-in-one Treasure Bucket

Buckle up, tiny explorers! Adventure awaits! We are about to explore, discover, collect, sense and observe. Who's ready for a treasure hunt? But what will you collect all your treasure in? A bag? A box? Or... what about an all-in-one reusable bucket? With the all-in-one bucket, your collected treasure will not be crushed, flattened or broken. It's so fun to carry around that A and G (my own tiny explorers) want to take it with us every time we go out.

Instructions:

1. Find a food container, preferably with a handle (we used a yoghurt pot, but you can also use an old lunch box or a biscuit tin).

2. Wrap the bucket in white paper. Use tape or double-sided tape to attach it to the container.

3. Make a hole on the upper part of the bucket and on the side of the lid, then thread a piece of string through them so the lid doesn't get lost easily.

4. Draw or use printed pictures of the items that you think you are going to find on your nature adventure (check tinynookplayground.com for templates).

5. Add a small box next to every object and tick it when found.

Develops: Patience, object and shape recognition and it also creates a sense of accomplishment and competition.

Other ideas: If laminated, it can also be used for tadpole hunting, rock pooling or crabbing.

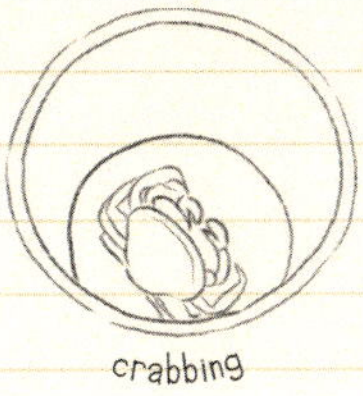

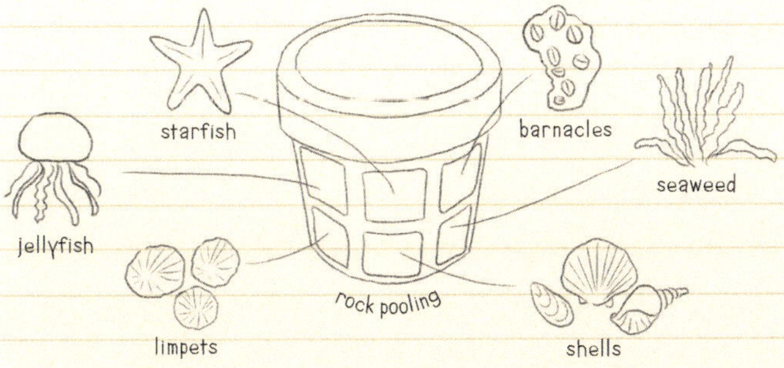

2. Plant Press

Herbariums (collection of dried plants) have been used with nature lovers for many years. Sometimes, books are used to help press flowers, but other flower-presses have been developed which make it a little less messy and helps keep books clean! The beauty of the pressed plants is that they can be used in several ways – you will find the plant press useful in many other activities that I will share with you within this book. This is going to be an invaluable asset in a tiny explorer's inventory.

Take it further: Decorate your press with pressed plants and flowers. Glue them with PVA glue and secure with varnish if you plan to take it outside on damp weather.

Instructions:

1. Cut plywood or thick cardboard into sizes of your choice for the covers of the press.

2. Carefully make a hole in each corner of the covers.

3. Prepare corrugated cardboard sheets for the interior of your press. These should be slightly smaller than the cover.

4. Cut the corners so they can properly fit between the holes.

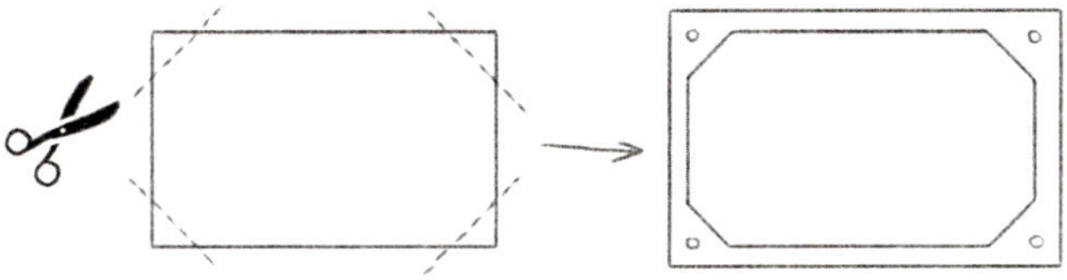

5. Place plants between the layers of cardboard, then fix them all together between the covers, add the screws and tighten the nuts.

6. It might take a few days before the plants are pressed, but you can check from time to time to see the progress.

Develops: Dexterity, patience and building skills.

Other ideas: You can still press plants between book pages. Use an old magazine or something you are not very attached to because plants might stain or wrinkle the pages. Put something heavy on top of your book/magazine so your plants can press properly.

Tip: Use wing nuts and screws if you plan to leave the press in the hands of tiny people. They would be easier to handle.

3. Windchime

A lucky clover, a feather for light sleep, a nut for the friendly squirrel or a cone just because. Whether for good luck, protection or decoration, windchimes can also be an expression of our personality. Ours was definitely enchanted with the gift of joy because after we hung it, the boys started running in circles making it tinkle and bursting into uncontrollable laughter.

Instructions:

1. Find a big twig to use as a base for your windchime.

2. Tie pieces of string at equal intervals. Make sure the string is a bit longer than the final length you would like to have.

3. Find all sorts of materials from nature to use as your swinging objects. We used leaves, flowers, feathers, cones and even moss. Rocks might not be the greatest idea though because they might untangle and hurt someone.

4. Make loops along the string to tie the objects. Insert the object into the loop and tighten the knot.

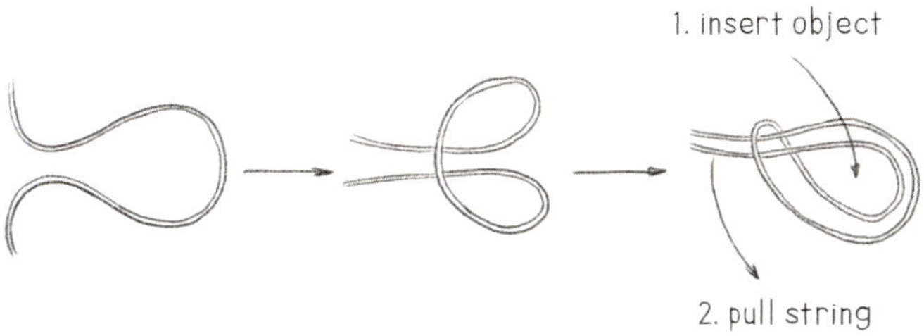

5. Place it somewhere you can see it, indoors or outdoors.

6. Enjoy watching it move when the wind blows.

Develops: The senses, hand-eye coordination, fine motor skills and social skills (if working on this with a friend).

Other ideas: You can also fix the strings on an embroidery hoop to make it look more interesting, or paint the objects to make it as colourful as you would like!

Tip: Use heavier objects on the bottom of the string so the string stays stretched.

4. Stick Frame Loom

The earliest evidence of a loom is around 4000 BC/Egypt, where it was used for clothes. But was it always intended for clothes? Maybe it was kids playing that gave grown-ups ideas? Let's go back in time and recreate the primordial stick frame loom together. Who knows what other ideas this activity might lead to!

Messiness Time Effort Theme

Instructions:

1. Make a square frame using 4 twigs tied together with string.

2. Wrap string all over the frame in one direction.

3. Start weaving plants between the strings until the entire area is filled with plants.

4. Add small details such as flowers, acorns, berries or alder cones.

5. Hang it in the desired place.

Develops: Fine motor skills, concentration, senses and hand-eye coordination.

Other ideas: Use flexible willow twigs or young pruned spring branches to weave a round frame instead of a square one.

Take it further: Make a vertical cuboid-shaped structure out of twigs and string and leave the bottom side unwoven. Put some Christmas lights inside and make a 'wild lamp' for your outdoor reading.

Tip: You can use evergreen plants and strawflowers to last longer.

5. Artsy Tree Installation

This is an activity very special to me as it is the one that showed how playing outside is great for a child's mind. It was actually A that came up with this idea. We were having a walk in the woods on a windy day. A was gathering lots of sticks and branches! 'A, what are you doing with those?' I asked him. 'I'm making a tree!' he replied. As bemused as I was, I didn't ask anymore and I watched as he used his imagination. He began arranging the sticks and branches to make them look like a tree. A 3D art installation! Little did I know, I was the next to get involved in this new activity – I really enjoyed it, I hope you do too.

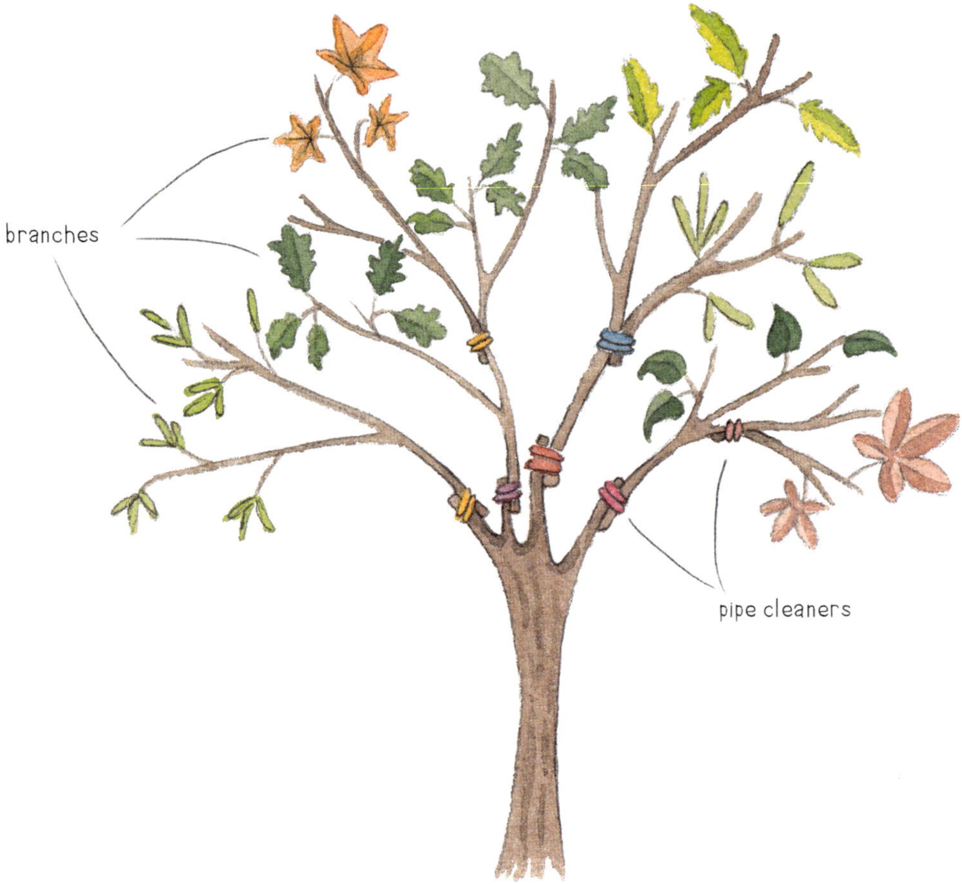

Instructions:

1. Use a knife or other sharp object to make a hole in the ground.

2. Fix a thick twig in the hole. This will be the trunk of your tree.

3. Start adding branches to your trunk and fasten them with string. Use pipe-cleaners or wire instead if you want to make it a little easier.

4. Add flowers or dried leaves close to the tips of the branches.

Develops: A sense of fun, imagination, motor skills and cognitive development.

Other ideas: Hang bird feeders onto the branches to attract garden birds.

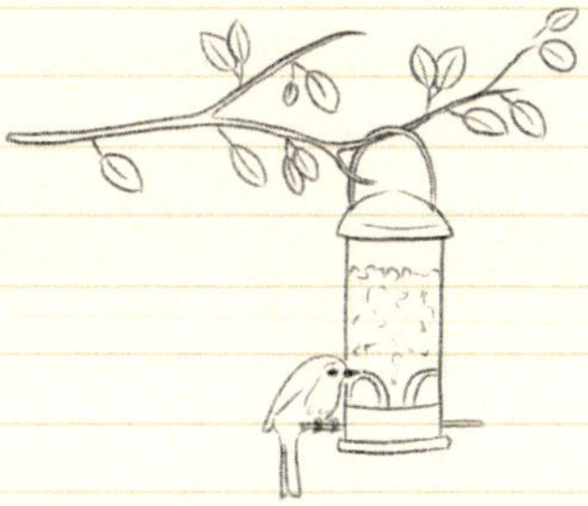

Fun fact: Grafting is a technique used by gardening experts to combine 2 plants. When done on trees, the result is having different fruits on the same plant.

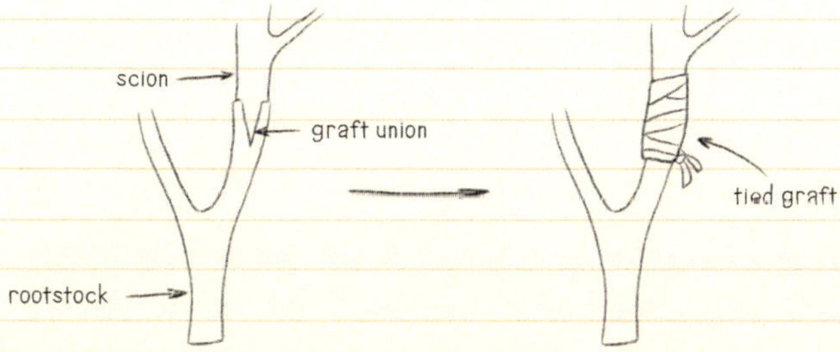

6. Divide and Contour

Our little explorers don't always need sophistication to be kept focused. This simple activity teaches shapes, numbers, grouping and sorting. It is also lots of fun – gathering the 'ingredients' is almost as fun as the activity itself!

Instructions:

1. Find a shady, dry spot where you can make the installation, it can be in your garden, in a park or a forest.

2. Make a grid out of twigs, with as many compartments as you like.

3. Start grouping all the things you have found into the created compartments.

4. Don't worry if you can't fill all of the compartments, you can do it on another day or maybe, if you create it in a park, your local community will add to your installation and it will surprise you when you return.

Develops: The senses, manipulation skills, a child's connection with nature and understanding of shapes.

Other ideas: Get creative and find other fun patterns for your installation.

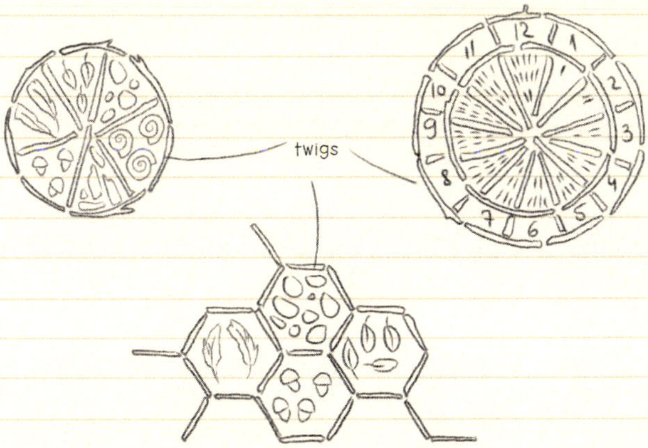

Fun fact: Acorns might disappear in a couple of hours. Munch! Munch!

7. Organic Teepee

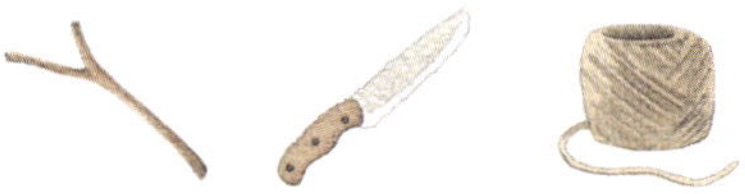

The fascination for tents, teepees and pillow forts that we had as kids must be somehow rooted in our nomadic ancestral genes since we feel incredibly safe as soon as we get inside one. Building one is another dual-purpose activity that has the potential of setting the scene for other great nature activities. We used some twigs from a tree that needed trimming in our garden, but you might find something lying around in a park or even some planks that Daddy's 'tomorrow project' never saw light.

Tip: Plant ivy or other climbing plants at the base of the branches if you want to keep it green for longer.

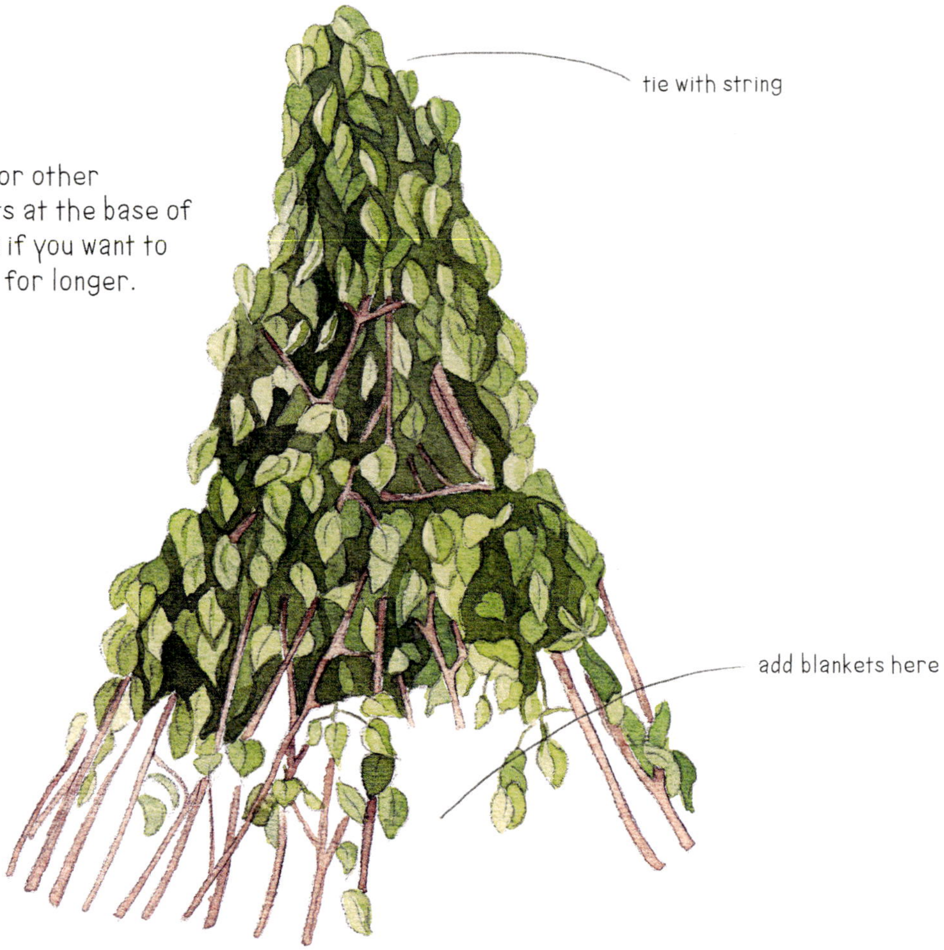

Instructions:

1. Gather about ten to twenty long branches of about the same size.

2. Use a knife to sharpen their tips so they would be easier to mount.

3. Tie 2 nails, one at each end of a string, and trace the diameter of your teepee on the ground.

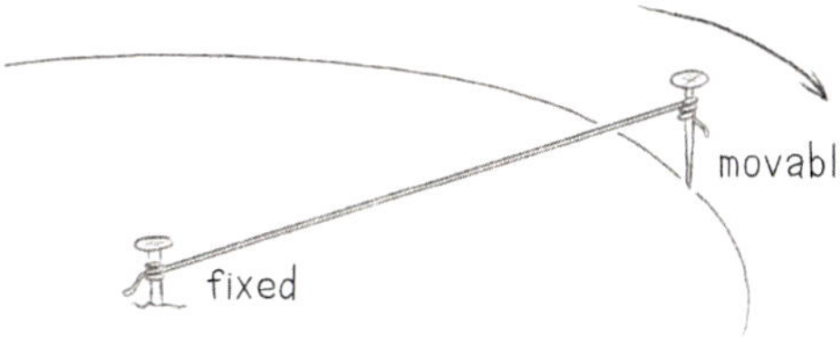

4. Make holes with a knife or other sharp object along the traced circle and stick the branches slightly angled to the inside of the circle.

5. Tie the other ends of the branches together with a piece of string to form a cone.

6. Cover with bed sheets if you want to make it shadier. Add blankets and pillows inside to make it cosy. And don't forget the books, so your little explorers can happily read in their own teepee.

Develops: Manipulative skills, teamwork, imagination and building skills.

Other ideas: Cover with Christmas lights and decorations in the wintertime.

Fun fact: Our teepee made a perfect shelter for a family of snails and they were really fun to watch.

8. Build it Up with Wood and Clay

Architecture helped people get out of caves and give form to their visions of a home. This was not an overnight success, but a long, tedious process that took centuries to perfect. This was the same for us – when we first started making our own huts we had a few errors! It began with us making a small garage for A's cars, but it blew away so we had to improve our design. With an improved technique, the results were better and many more ideas came after. We built houses, bridges, garages and castles for our favourite toys and we let the stories unfold.

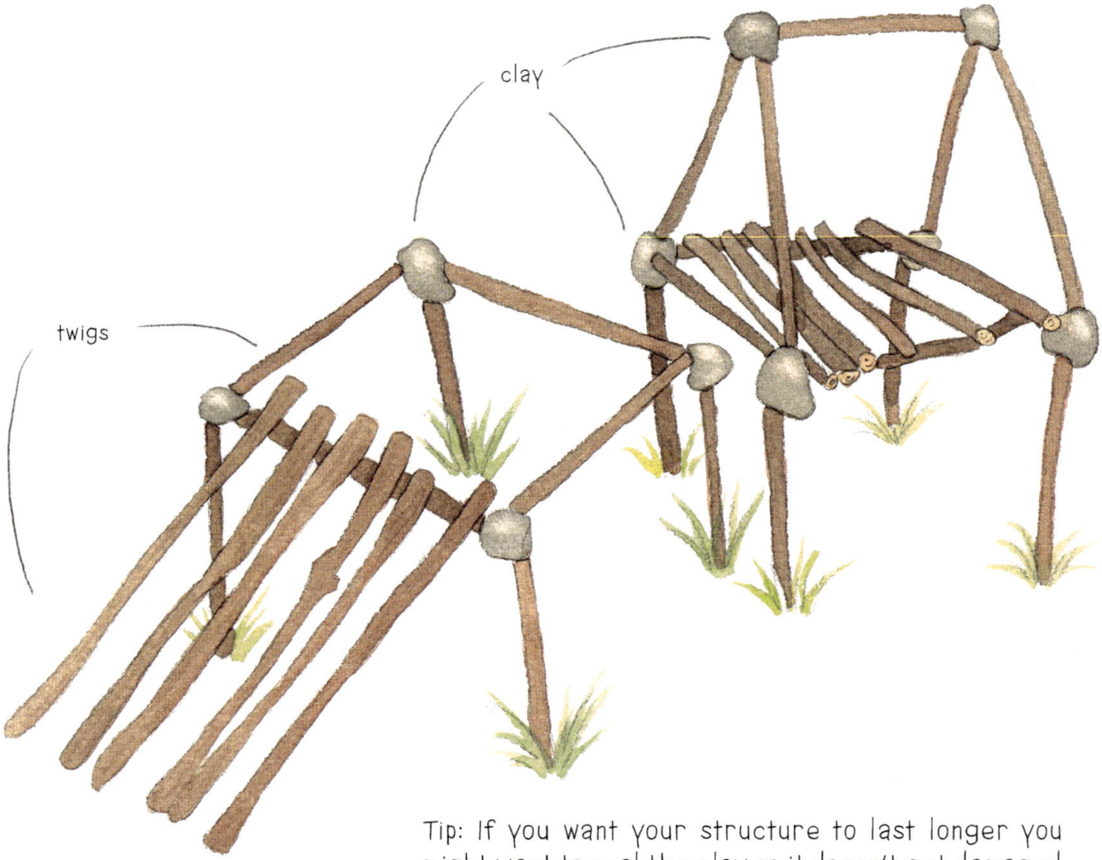

Tip: If you want your structure to last longer you might want to seal the clay so it doesn't get damaged by the rain. Use a coat of varnish or acrylic paint to cover the clay after it dries out completely.

Instructions:

1. Collect twigs and break them to pieces of about the same size.

2. Use a sharp object to make holes in the ground and stick 4 twigs to start your 3D structure.

3. Model some clay balls and stick them on the top of the twigs.

4. Now, fix 4 twigs on top of them horizontally to make a square.

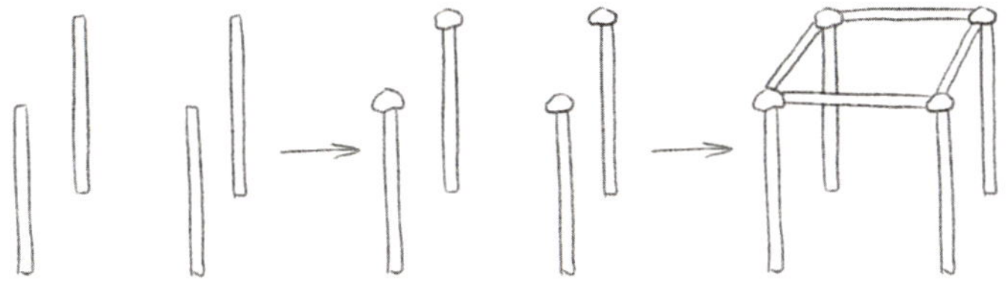

5. Create a platform by placing lots of twigs on the layer you created. Continue your structure as you wish.

Develops: Play skills, problem-solving, creativity, learning through mistakes and concentration.

Other ideas: Go wild – create houses, pyramids, blocks of flats, castles, ramps and connect them together with bridges and tunnels.

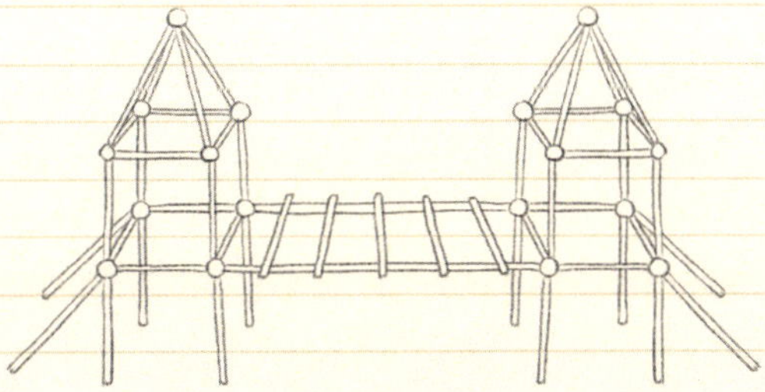

9. Forest Bazaar

Our tiny little explorers can now present their treasures gathered during their wild expeditions and create a marketplace to sell them! Have your child search carefully for the finest produce to showcase in their shop. Encourage them to barter and haggle like the finest sellers did in ancient times. Paper money can be super-fun to make too. Have family members and friends join in and then enjoy counting the profits... these profits could fund the next expeditions!

Instructions:

1. Go outside and gather lots of different things for your shop: plants, berries, seeds, cones, rocks.

2. Sort them in food containers or small boxes and add price tags to them.

3. Fold paper cones and fill them with the goodies bought from the shop.

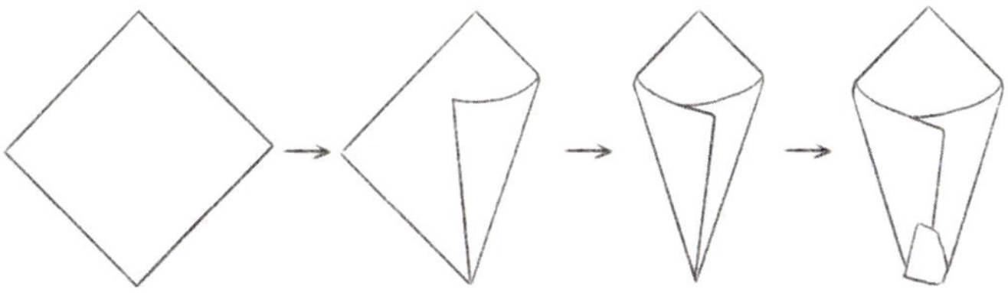

4. Prepare paper money and buttons as currency for the shop.

5. Take turns being the seller in order to engage in dialogue and, why not, negotiate the price.

Develops: Social interaction, communication, imagination and counting.

Other ideas: Use a scale to weigh the ingredients if you have one at hand.

Tip: Reuse! Some of the things bought from the shop would make good ingredients for the next/another activity.

10. It's Munch-time!

May I present you one of the most popular pretend games brought to you... with an organic twist. Tiny explorers found delicious ingredients during their journeys and also exchanged a few at the markets. World-class chefs, brace yourselves, tiny chefs are about to revolutionise the world cuisine with yummy forest ingredients.

Instructions:

1. Have your ingredients ready and decide what recipe you are going to 'cook'.

2. Use tools like a knife or scissors to cut the ingredients (or you could use your hands to break and tear them).

3. Mix the ingredients, add water and stir. Or just stack them to make a sandwich.

4. Use fancy kitchen phrases like 'al dente rocks', 'bechamel clay' or 'julienne twigs' to make it more fun.

5. You can even pretend you have your own cooking show. What would it be called?

6. Feed everyone.

Develops: Dexterity and ability to follow instructions.

Other ideas: Make cards with recipes and ask the kids to make a certain dish.

PIZZA CON NATURA

Ingredients:
- 1 clay dough
- 4 cut leaves
- 6 dandelion flowers
- 10 small rocks
- 1 tbsp rainwater
- moss for topping
- a pinch of sand

Method: Knead the dough until soft. Roll the dough and add the ingredients. Set under the sun and cook until it's crusty. Enjoy!

Take it further: Take photos of your favourite meals or find interesting ones online and try to reproduce the colouring and arrangement of the plating, with the natural ingredients. Reuse an old ketchup bottle and fill it with mud for those artsy plate lines.

11. Sail Away

It's time to explore across the waters and find new territories the way the big maritime explorers did. Paper boats are a good introduction to sailing, but can only take us so far as they get soaked and sink rather quickly. In this task, we flex our skills to build boats that will astonish even the most demanding... ducks on the lake.

Instructions:

1. Use a hand drill to make a hole in the centre of a piece of tree bark.

2. Glue a twig in the hole and attach a leaf to it. Optionally, paint the leaf beforehand.

3. Make another smaller hole on one end of the boat.

4. Get a long piece of string through the hole to tie the boat and wrap the loose end around a twig.

5. Launch it into a pond, a lake or... the bathtub.

Develops: Manipulative skills and the understanding of cause and effect.

Other ideas: Release your boat on a river instead of a lake or pond to make it more fun. Unwind the string to let the boat go further from you and wind it in to bring the boat back.

Take it further: Make a race! Build more boats, paint numbers on the sails, create a finish line then remove the string and release them. See which boat wins the race.

12. The King of the Wild

After conquering the unexplored lands over the seas, the forest creatures saw a long-awaited ruler in our tiny explorer. Kings and queens of lands of might and magic, welcome a new leader! The righteous and wise, caring and mindful King said: 'Miss Fox and Mister Mouse, you are to shake paws, forget the past!'

Instructions:

1. For the crown: Measure your child's head circumference and cut a piece of cardboard a little wider than that and about 20cm (8in) in height.

2. Cover your rectangle with double-sided tape.

3. Draw some zig-zags on one side of the cardboard and cut them off.

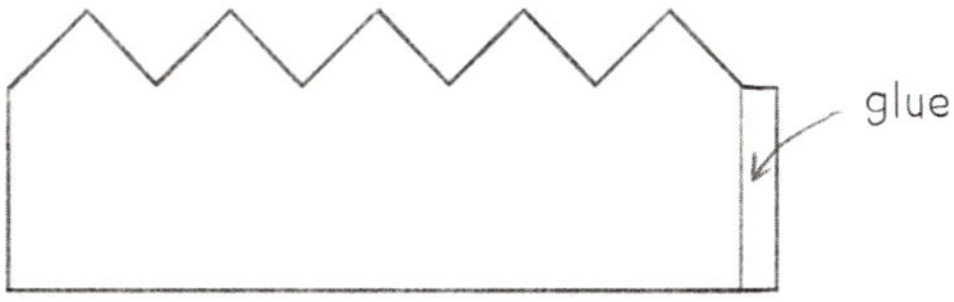

4. Glue the ends together to make a crown.

5. Whilst outside, peel off the tape protection and stick leaves and plants to the crown until the whole surface is covered.

6. Find a nice twig for the 'staff'.

7. Gather a bunch of plants of your choice.

8. Hold them together and use string or rubber band to attach them to the tip of the twig.

Develops: Imagination, dexterity, motor skills and hand-eye coordination.

Other ideas: Try other stories like Princess of the Wild or Witch/Wizard of the Wild.

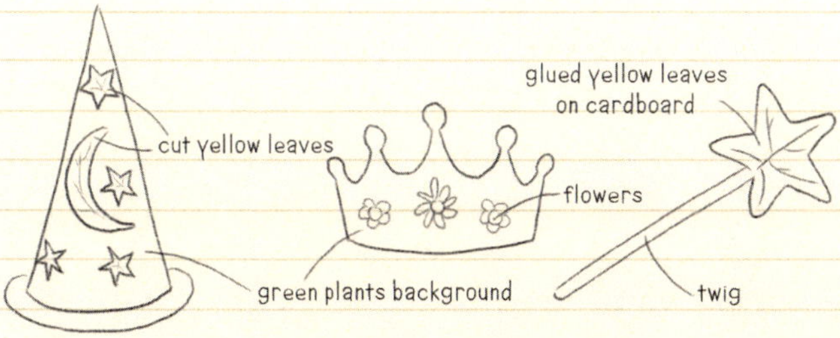

13. This Little Bear

... Went to market, this little bear stayed home. Bears and Cubs Fan Club's top member, G, was really excited during this activity. Pick your favourite teddies and start reading them stories. Bears not really your thing? With a few tweaks and use of other materials like feathers, helicopter seeds, twigs, acorn caps for ears and noses, you can bring to life all your story friends.

Instructions:

1. Carve big enough holes in each horse-chestnut for the fingers to fit in.

2. Make some small cuttings for the ears and insert cone scales in them. Be extra careful!

3. Use a black marker to draw eyes, nose and mouth on the lighter part of the chestnut. You can also use white paint to add some highlights.

4. Put them on your fingers and tell a bunch of made-up stories.

Develops: Imaginative play and creativity.

Other ideas: Make different kinds of animals and set up a cardboard puppet theatre.

Tip: You can use balls of clay instead of chestnuts if they are not in season.

14. Chief Officer Stick

String puppets, also known as marionettes, entertained us for ages and ages, maybe even before theatres with actors appeared. Due to its playful nature, I like to think that it might've been an ancient tiny explorer who first came up with a prototype of a string puppet. I present you, Chief Officer Stick, second in command. The most helpful companion and a most trusted friend.

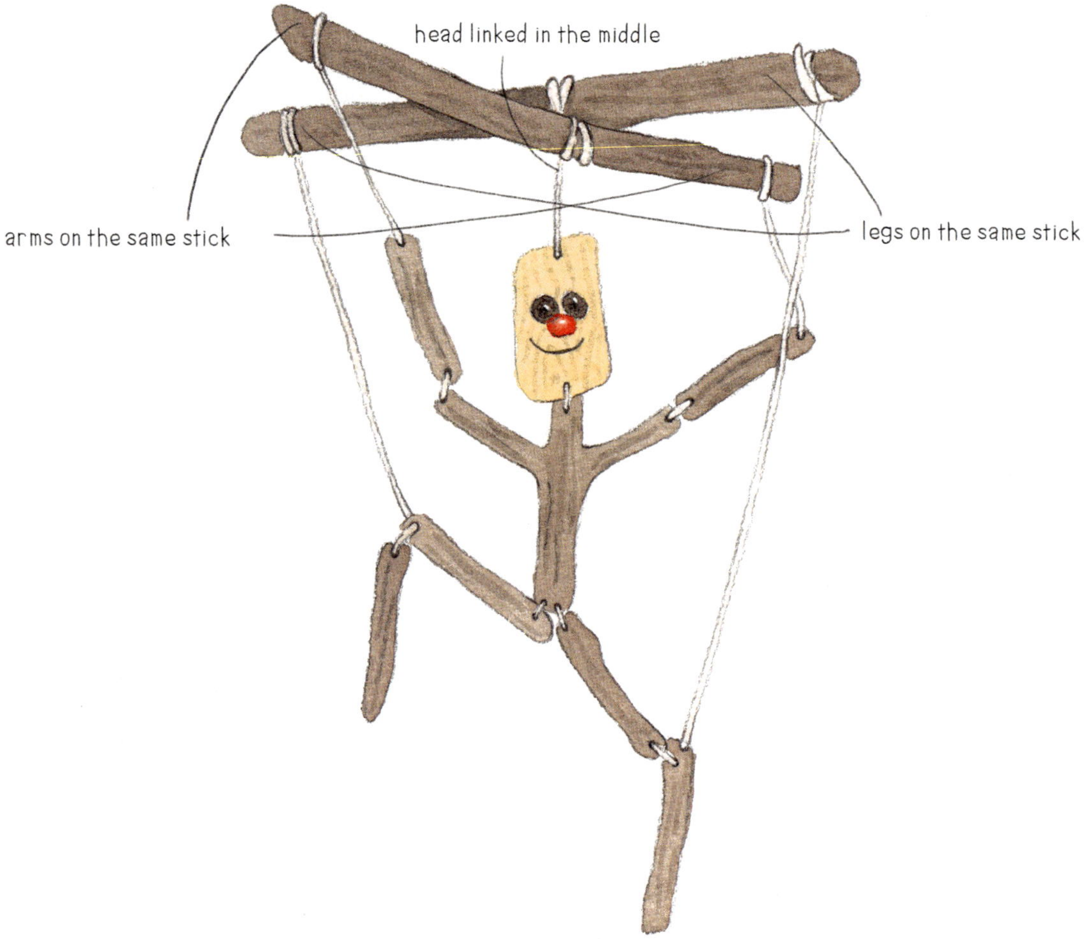

Instructions:

1. Find some straight twigs to use for the arms and legs of your puppet. For the head, you can use a thicker twig, a piece of bark or a slice of wood.

2. Drill holes at the end of every twig and hold the twigs together with string (make sure the knot is loose enough so the pieces can move independently).

3. Use a piece of string to tie together two twigs in a cross-shaped handle.

4. Make sure the arms are on the ends of the same stick and leg joints are on the ends of the other stick (check illustration on the left).

5. Link the centre of the cross to the head with another piece of string.

6. Adjust the string dimensions so that the puppet will move whenever you rotate the cross.

7. Create the puppet's face by drawing with a marker or using objects from nature for the nose, eyes and mouth.

Develops: Understanding of cause and effect (when you move the cross handle in a certain way, the puppet moves accordingly), imagination, coordination and building skills.

Other ideas: Add bells on his legs and arms for an auditory sensory experience. Also, check the next activity for a new idea.

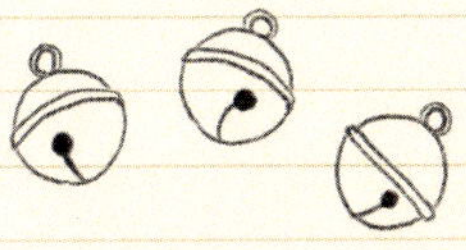

15. Cut, Paste and Dry

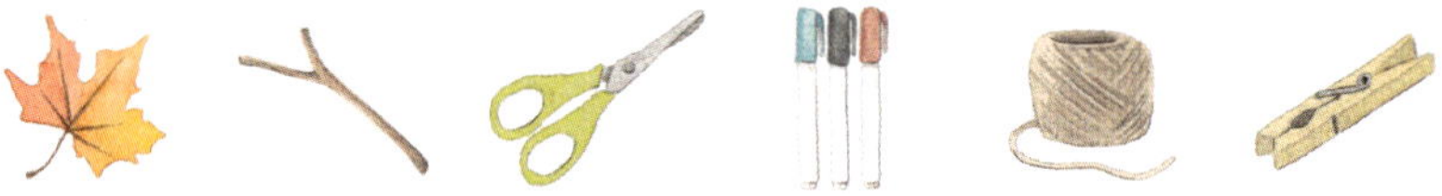

These long adventures into unknown lands ask for a well-deserved break. Let's make camp next to a river and wash our (tiny) clothes. Access to tumble dryers is strictly restricted. Who would've thought that chores can actually be this fun?

Instructions:

1. Use a knife or other sharp object to make two holes in the ground.

2. Fix two twigs in the holes and lay a string between them to resemble a washing line.

3. Use a marker to draw clothes onto thick leaves and then cut them with scissors.

4. Use pegs to hang the clothes on the line.

Develops:	Fine motor skills, creativity and understanding the real world.
Other ideas:	Use different coloured leaves for socks and try matching them afterwards.
Take it further:	Sew clothes for Chief Officer Stick. Create two shirt patterns from big leaves. No big leaves? Use paper instead. Make holes at the edge of the shirt with a hole punch and sew the two pieces together with flower stems.

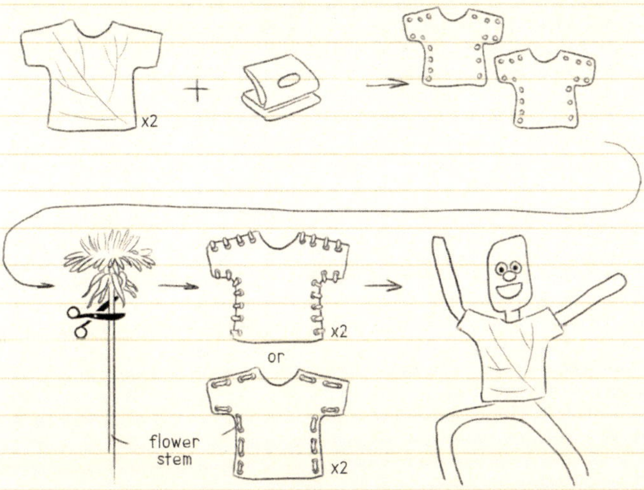

16. Map of the Wild

All expeditions would be useless without good cartographers, the people who make maps. Coastlines and high mountains, cliffs and deep caves, all need to be very carefully marked on a map. Use this activity to unleash the inner cartographer and careful landscapist, and give life to places of wonder. You can even hide pirate treasures somewhere. Shh, don't tell the secret to anyone!

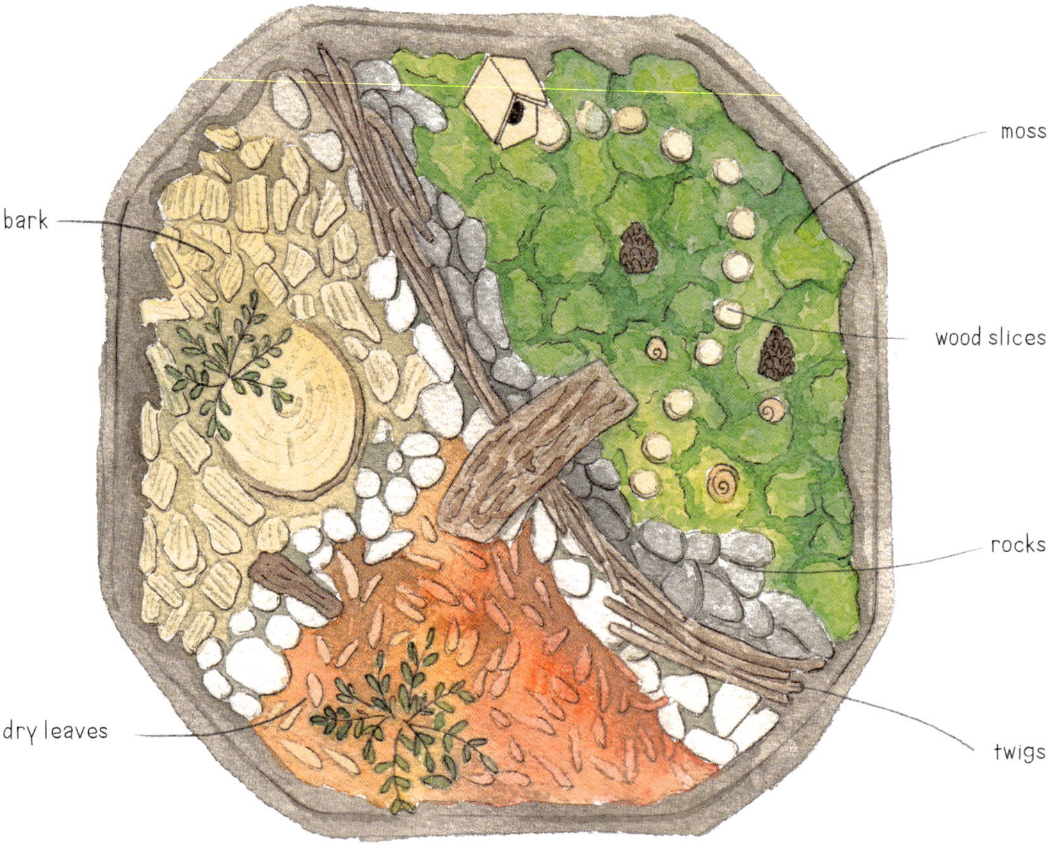

Instructions:

1. Gather lots of nature things.

2. Find a tray and decide about what everything should be. We went big but smaller trays would work too.

3. You can use moss for the green fields, twigs for the river (you can even paint them blue), rocks for the mountains, dry leaves for the woods. Use bark to make bridges across the river or caves for the wild animals to hide in.

4. Bring toys to play. We almost always use toy wild animals to play with, but we sometimes create a cosy, natural environment for the toy cars.

Develops: Imagination, building skills, language and independent play.

Other ideas: Make bushes from small leafy branches stuck in a clay base.

Take it further: Create animals too. Use a ball of clay for the body, small twigs for the legs, make fur textures and add small details like twig antlers or red berry noses.

17. Nuts about Food

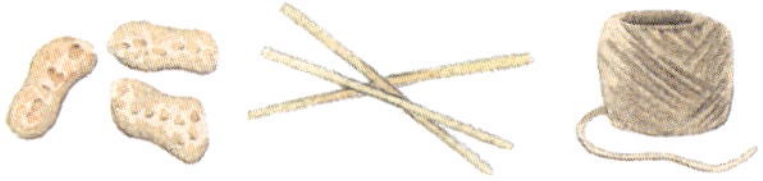

My children love fruit kebabs. They like both making, and eating them! Making nut kebabs is just as fun as making fruit ones. We all know squirrels like nuts but they go nuts about nut kebabs. The first part will be preparing the kebabs, then building the luring teepee and then patiently observing. For the more tech-oriented explorers, install a sensor activated camera nearby to get everything on tape while observing from afar.

Instructions:

1. Use the sharp end of a barbecue stick to bead the peanuts onto it.

2. Fill about four sticks making sure you leave them empty at the ends.

3. Insert one end of every stick in the ground at a slight angle so that it would resemble a teepee. Secure the other ends together with string or rubber bands.

4. Set up a camera to see who will visit your garden to enjoy the tasty kebabs! You could build a hide if you think you are patient enough to wait.

Develops: Patience, hand-eye coordination and dexterity.

Other ideas: You can make a similar one with apples for the birds. But make sure you hang it in a tree instead of putting it on the ground. Birds feel much safer if they are able to look for predators.

Take it further: Don't have a camera? Place a tray filled with damp sand or flour and set your feeder inside. You'll still be able to find out who visited by checking for footprints in the sand.

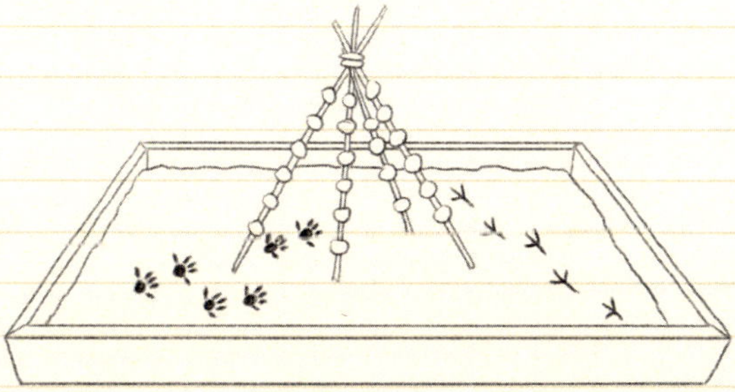

Fun fact: Moist cat food might attract foxes or hedgehogs (or... cats) during the night.

18. Seed Garland

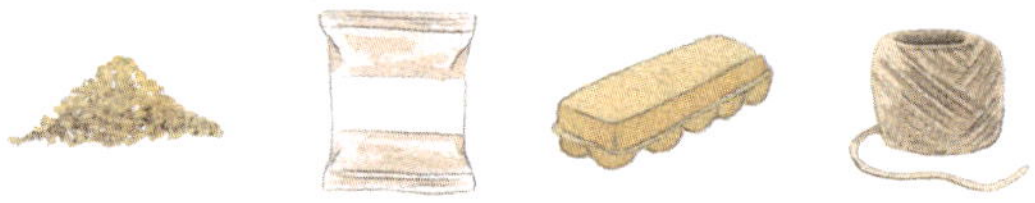

When new, unexplored habitats are found, the amount of new species discovered is incredible. Knowing the techniques to feed and attract birds is important. Bird feeders come in all shapes and forms. It's rewarding for birds to find food without needing to dig too much for a change. Feeding birds teaches kids to be considerate and careful with the creatures of the wild but also gives them the opportunity to study these delightfully coloured creatures.

Instructions:

1. Mix bird seeds with food gelatin (follow the instructions on the gelatin packet to make sure you add the right amount of water). You don't want to add too much gelatin – just enough to make the seeds stick to each other.

2. Pour the mix in some moulds (we used quail egg boxes but you can use regular egg boxes, ice trays or silicone moulds).

3. Place a thread of string on top of the mixture and add a new layer of the mix on top of it, leaving the ends of the string a little bit longer.

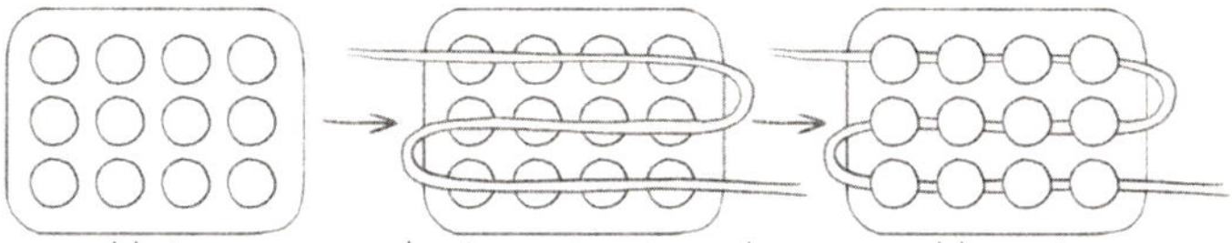

a. add the mix   b. place the thread   c. add new layer

4. Put in the fridge for a few hours until it hardens.

5. Take the garland out of the mould and hang it in a place of your choice. Wait for the birds to find the treat and enjoy watching them.

Develops: Senses, imagination, dexterity, kindness and knowledge of birds.

Other ideas: Make a log with all the birds that visited your garden, find out their names and learn a fact or two about them.

Date	Type of bird	Number spotted	Fun facts
24.05	Goldcrest	2	The smallest bird in the UK
29.05	Starling	3	Can mimic alarm sounds
4.06	Jay	1	Belongs to the crow family
4.06	Robin	7	Can sing at night

19. Tiny Wormery

We owe so much to these tiny creatures that we mainly get to see after the rain. Worms are responsible for increasing the amount of air and water in the ground and naturally fertilise the soil. Farmers even create wormeries for the purpose of turning household waste into compost that is full of nutrients, which is then used for growing much healthier plants. This activity allows you to see up-close the process through which worms transform the soil within a tiny wormery.

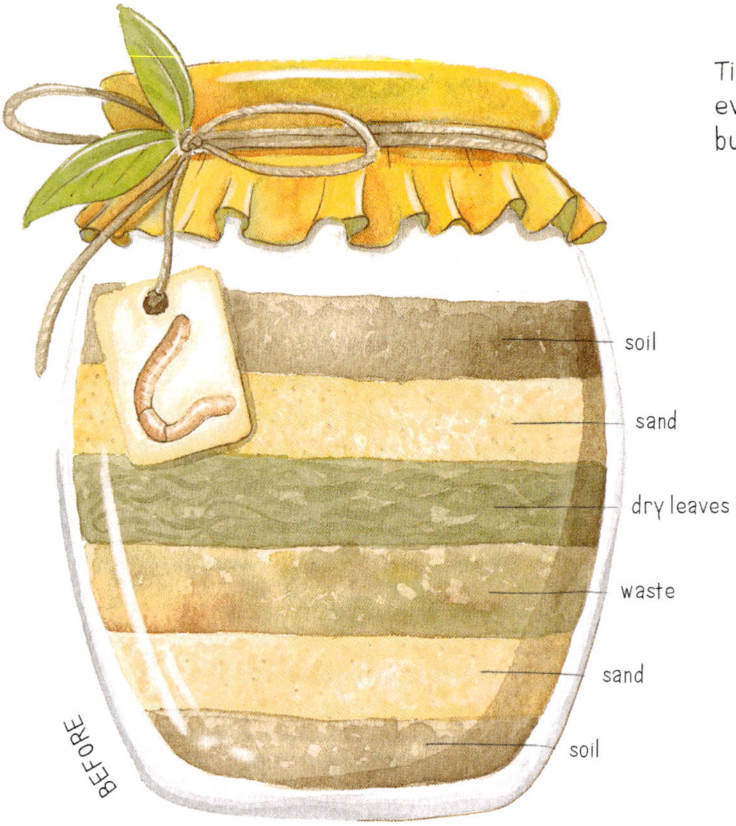

Tip: Add some small pieces of food every day (vegetables or fruits, but avoid onion and citrus).

Instructions:

1. Find a transparent container – we used a plastic bottle with the top cut off. Make small holes on the bottom to help drain the excess water.

2. Fill the container with layers of sand, soil, dry leaves, waste (vegetables, fruits, coffee grounds, tea bags, paper or cardboard). It doesn't matter if you don't have all of the ingredients.

3. Add a small amount of water after every added layer to keep it moist.

4. Collect about five medium-sized worms, put them on top of the mixture and cover the container with fabric. They will start digging towards the bottom of the jar as soon as you place them inside!

5. Cover the container in card so no light will get through and place your jar in a shady spot.

6. Check daily to see if the worms have managed to mix together all the layers.

7. Make sure you release the worms after they have transformed the layers into compost and you have made your observations.

Develops: Curiosity and understanding of the world.

Other ideas: Try making a time-lapse by taking multiple photos a day, for several days from the exact same spot.

Take it further: Reuse the fertile soil to grow something.

Fun fact: Worms love watermelons.

20. Creepy-Crawlies Hotel

Bees, beetles, centipedes, millipedes, spiders, snails, woodlice. Welcome to the Tiny World of Tiny Beasts. Bug hotels can shelter many friendly creepy-crawlies as well as flying ones. Whether big or small, as this will depend on the resources at hand, the hotel will soon become a busy place for tiny creatures. Don't forget to take your magnifying glass.

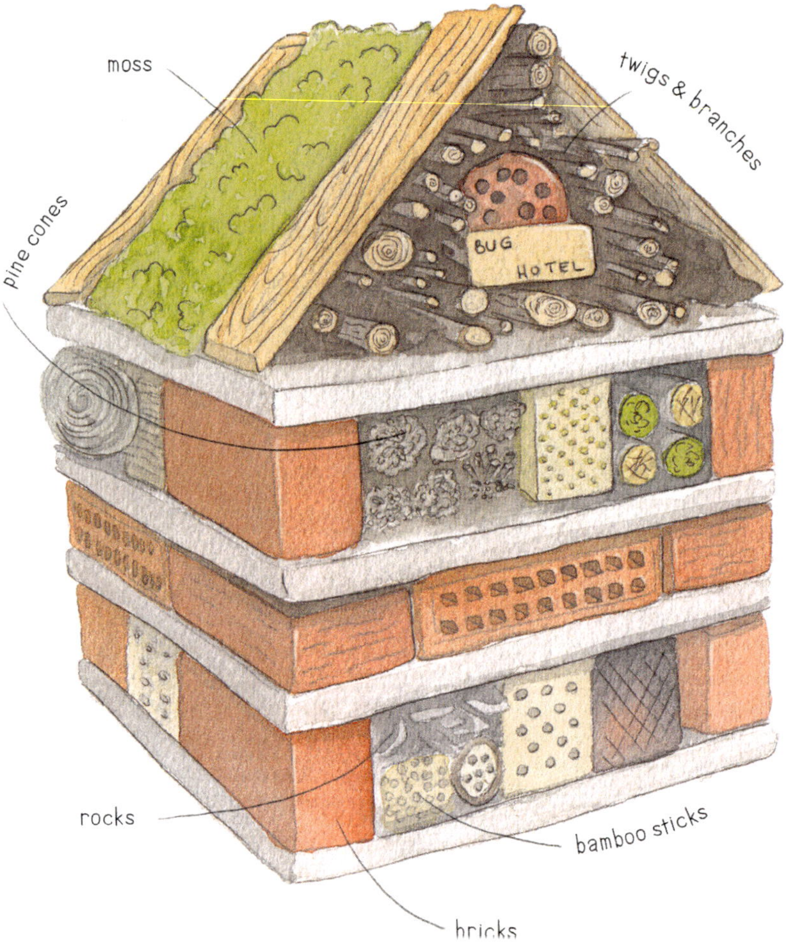

Fun fact: Lesser stag beetles are great 'hotel' builders. They make holes in rotten wood or tree stumps and live most of their lives there. Look for holes in old tree stumps. The beetles usually come out at dawn as they are nocturnal creatures, but you may spot one if you're lucky!

Instructions:

1. Make a sturdy structure out of wood pellets, bricks, wooden planks, or anything else you find suitable.

2. Make some compartments and fill the nooks with things you have at hand. It can be twigs, rotten wood, pine cones, rocks, tree bark, straw. Hollow bamboo sticks are bees' favourite. While spiders prefer the cosiness of dry leaves to lay their eggs in, woodlice like moist logs. We even used PVC pipes filled with straw and moss, wood boards with drilled holes in them, corrugated cardboard and rolled carpet scraps.

3. Wait for a few days and you'll soon see some new residents moving in.

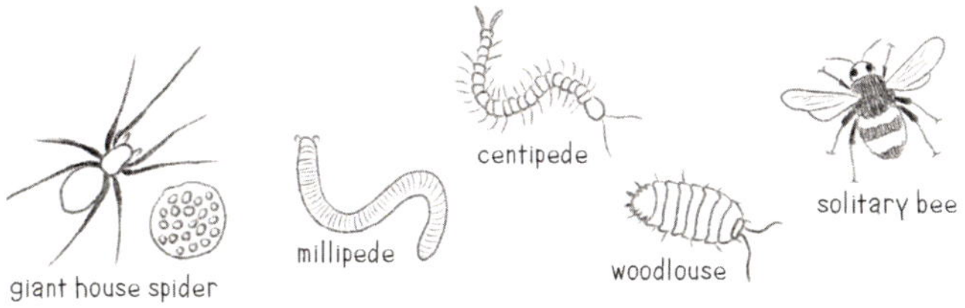

4. Watch them from a distance and keep a log of who visits.

5. Shhh, try not to disturb them once they are all settled in!

Develops: Kindness and consideration, building skills, fine motor skills, patience and decision-making.

Other ideas: Line up chunky rotten logs in a moist, shady area of your garden, wait for a few days, then give the kids a magnifying glass to check out the new inhabitants under the logs.

21. Flower Mosaic

There are many mosaics that decorate the halls and walls of famous buildings but, unfortunately, it's mostly a dying art due to the level of detail and time it takes to create. Let your tiny artist come up with a new arrangement for the dining table, something for that corner in the living room. For us, the measure of success with this activity was A calling for Daddy, 'Look, Daddy, I've made a flower car with flower wheels!'

Instructions:

1. Decide on whether you are going to use a tea strainer or a regular colander for this project.

2. Use flowers and other plants to fill in the holes of your strainer.

3. You can use a single type of flower (daisies or buttercups would work just fine) or play with different colours. You can make letters or show off your drawing skills by placing the plants in many different shapes.

4. If you are feeling very creative you can also make some mandala-like patterns.

Develops: Creativity and concentration, fine motor skills and hand-eye coordination.

Other ideas: If you'd like your arrangement to stay fresh a little longer, leave the flower stems longer and place the strainer on top of a bowl filled with water.

Tip: Use dried flowers instead of regular plants to make it last forever.

22. Clay Imprints

Clay. So inexpensive, so easy to find, so simple, yet so versatile. Clay helped us give form to our visions in the early ages and supported us in building shelter. The uses of clay were, and still are, so broad that there are countless books about it. My little ones love playing with it. One of the most popular activities for us is leaving imprints on clay. They make nice gifts too.

Instructions:

1. Use a rolling pin to stretch the clay. Make it about 5mm (0.2in) thick so it won't break easily after it hardens.

2. Find all sorts of plants, cones, feathers, shells (anything could work really), and push them a little into the clay. Use the rolling pin again if you want to push them evenly.

3. Use tweezers to remove the bits that are hard to remove by hand.

4. Make it look more interesting by adding layers of cut-out clay with imprinted leaves on it.

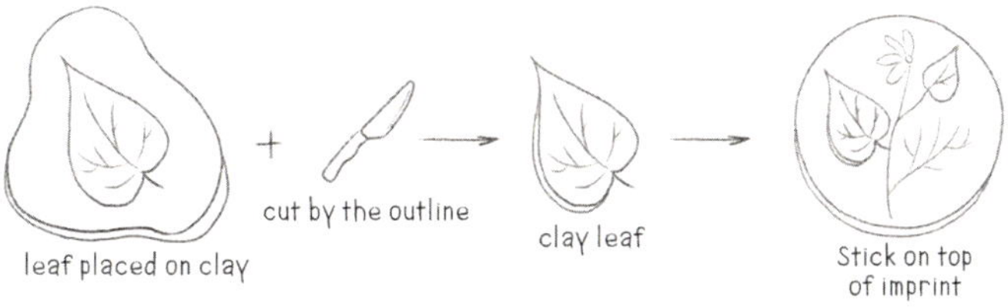

5. Use glossy varnish to seal or acrylic paint to give some colour after it dries.

Develops: Senses, dexterity, fine motor skills and promotes relaxation.

Other ideas: Use toys to leave imprints in clay and play a game of finding out who left the imprints (toy animals, car tyres, stamps).

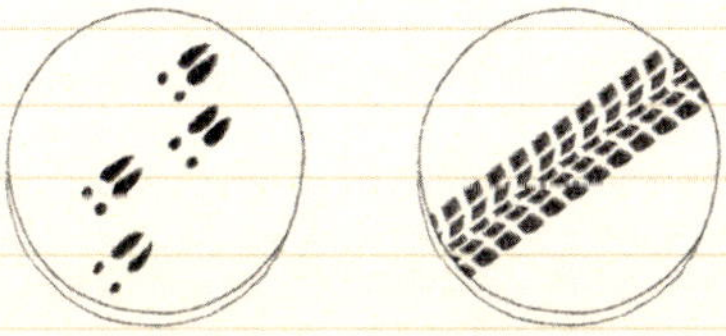

Tip: Imprint tiny hands to make keepsake memories for when the kids get older.

23. Clay Creatures

Kids in early times didn't have the huge amounts of toys we have today, so they had to be inventive. Next time you visit a museum, look at the exhibits of clay toys and appreciate the level of detail. But until then, let's make our own and then display it on a tree – if you like. Do you want more exposure? Create it at home and then take it to a park or forest tree for others to enjoy.

Instructions:

1. Find a tree that you think would be good for your creature to sit on.

2. Collect lots of natural materials to use later on: bark, twigs, acorns, lichen.

3. Use a lump of clay as a base and stick it to the tree trunk.

4. Model the clay in the shape of a head or body and add features to it using the natural materials.

5. Let your imagination run wild – create hedgehogs with spiky backs using lots of small twigs or burdock seeds, majestic deers with huge antlers, monsters with terrible rocky teeth and huge noses, scary spiders with long legs and lots of eyes or fairies with long grassy hair and acorn earrings.

Develops: Concentration, creativity, imagination and ability to express feelings.

Other ideas: If you feel like creating clay creatures when it's a really bad weather outside, you can still create them indoors. Make some scratchy marks on the back of your creature after you finish and wait for it to dry. When it's time to stick it to the tree, just spread some clay over the scratched area and attach your creature to the tree. All done!

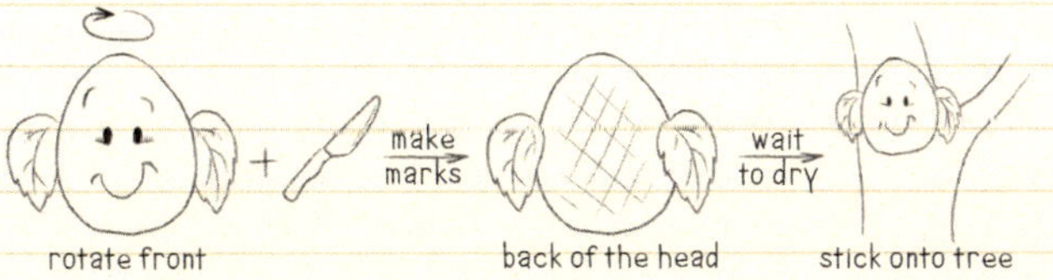

Tip: Use cookie cutters to make different patterns and decorate the tree. Seal the clay with varnish or acrylic paint after it dries out, to make it last a little longer.

24. Rock-Paper-Flowers

We all have bad days every now and then. Imagine how difficult and frustrating it is for the little ones. Sometimes, we just want to blow off some steam! An occasional rough and tumble, throwing pillows and other high-energy activities are good ways to let out tension and release energy. Letting out these feelings of frustration is really important, and this activity sets out to help children express these difficult-to-cope-with emotions, whilst also creating wonderful art.

Instructions:

1. Gather flowers and plants of different colours.

2. Find a really smooth rock to use as a hammer.

3. Fold a piece of white card in half.

4. Insert some of your plants between the fold and use the rock to smash the plants inside.

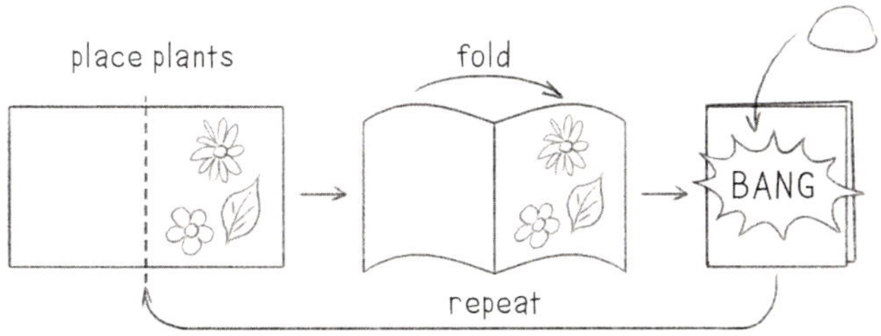

5. Open from time to time to check the outcome. Add other plants, arrange them in different patterns and hammer some more.

Develops: The ability to regulate emotions and resilience against stress and adversity.

Other ideas: Use a white t-shirt instead of paper. Place a card inside the t-shirt. Place the flowers and plants on top and put it between 2 pieces of card. Use the rock again to print the plants onto the t-shirt.

Tip: Cut the paper on the fold line. Now you have two similar artworks that you can frame and exhibit or give as a gift.

25. Sticky Picture

The emptiness of a new canvas frightens me a bit every single time... until the first spot of colour. This must be an adult problem as the little ones have no issue in filling in any type, and I mean ANY type, of surface in an instant without that need for the first drop. Maybe it is because their beautiful minds are an ever-spinning rainbow of ideas? A and G had loads of fun with this activity. You can try repeating the activity every 3 months to see your child's capacity of absorbing information and mirroring it in the form of art.

Instructions:

1. Use a wood frame or craft one from cardboard by cutting out a rectangle.

2. Turn the frame upside down and stick a piece of contact paper onto the frame (sticky part will be on the front). You can also use strips of tape instead of contact paper.

3. Use flat nature elements to decorate the 'canvas'.

4. Your artwork is already in a frame so one thing less to worry about, just hang it on the wall and enjoy it.

Develops: The right side of the brain, non-verbal communication and self-expression.

Other ideas: Create circular patterns and letters or use your imagination to 'draw' beautiful scenes or creatures.

Take it further: Build a tape net by randomly fixing a few twigs in the ground and laying tape between them. Every time you enter the net you get to add something new on the tape. Take turns and move at a fast pace making sure you don't get stuck inside.

Tip: Use pressed plants for a design that lasts a little longer.

26. Reverse Stencil

Do you like stencils? This task is just like a stencil but in reverse. Instead of filling in a pattern, it's the shape that remains white, whilst the rest gets flooded with wonderful colour. Mix them in any possible way and be amazed by the results. You could use watercolours as well, but we used food colouring for simplicity and because this way it's edible... not saying we have tried (wink).

Instructions:

1. Fill spray bottles with water and some droplets of food colouring. Shake well.

2. Arrange some plants, leaves or flowers in different positions on a piece of card.

3. Place a rock on top of every plant to keep them in place during the process.

4. Use the spray bottles to spray coloured water onto the paper.

5. Wait until the paint dries then lift up the plants to discover the outcome.

Develops: Understanding of colours, confidence, memory and vision.

Other ideas: You can repeat the process once again, overlapping plants on the same piece of card for more complex results.

Take it further: Mix some water, food colouring and liquid soap into a small, shallow bowl. Dip a bubble wand or a straw into the mix and blow coloured soap bubbles on top of your card with the plants placed on top. They will leave interesting patterns When they pop on the paper .

Tip: Use pressed plants. They sit better on the paper, resulting in better-looking shapes.

27. Nature Children

Unlike the rest of the activities which are meant to keep the little ones interested and engaged, this one is my gift to you for all the patience you have had in spite of all the trouble I've put you through! Speaking for myself, I just wanted to remember this period when my children were so enthusiastic about everything, when they wanted to explore and were super excited with every new discovery.

Instructions:

1. Take a picture of your child's profile and print it.

2. Cut the profile and use it to trace the outline onto a piece of card.

3. Cut out the profile from the card.

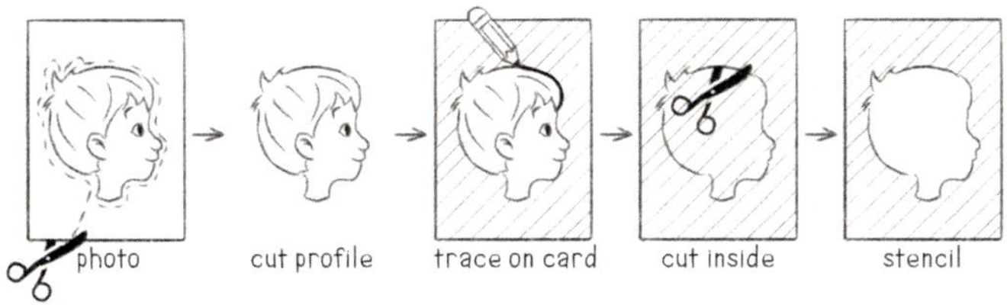

4. Stick some double-sided tape onto a new piece of card, the same size as the previous one, until you cover it all up. You can also use glue but the card might wrinkle a bit.

5. Remove the tape protection, and start sticking pressed plants, until all the card is fully covered.

6. Cut any excess plants that have gone past the side of the card.

7. Stick the profile stencil on top of the decorated card and frame the resulted portrait.

Develops: Social skills, communication, self-confidence, fine motor skills, dexterity and improves hand-eye coordination.

Tip: Your plants should be pressed really well and be fully dry if you want to put glass on top of your picture, otherwise the glass and the moisture from the leaf might create mold afterwards due to the humidity inside.

28. Bird Nest

Birds are master weavers. They have the ability to build intricate structures, nests made of a thousand pieces of dry grass, weaved one by one within a day. Did you spot any during your walks, maybe with the binoculars? Be sure to keep a distance from them though as Mummy Birdie might get scared and not come back to the nest. Instead, we could try and replicate one and get to learn and appreciate the great nest-building abilities the birds have.

Instructions:

1. Use a small pile of straw and model it to resemble a bird nest.

2. Try making a ring out of some flexible branches (E.g. willow) and weave the straw or dry grass around it – some types of birds do this.

3. After your structure is sturdy enough, add some small feathers (birds add them for insulation, to keep them warm), alder cones, birch bark or moss to make it stronger and camouflaged.

4. Find some egg-shaped rocks and put them inside the nest.

5. You can even paint the rocks if you think they would look prettier.

6. Fix your nest on a tree branch or use it inside as a decorative piece.

Develops: Coordination, patience and perseverance.

Other ideas: Help bird conservation by building a nest-box

Fun fact: Different types of birds create nests differently, some birds even use mud or saliva to build their nests. The desert-dwelling woodpecker spends months building its nest in a cactus.

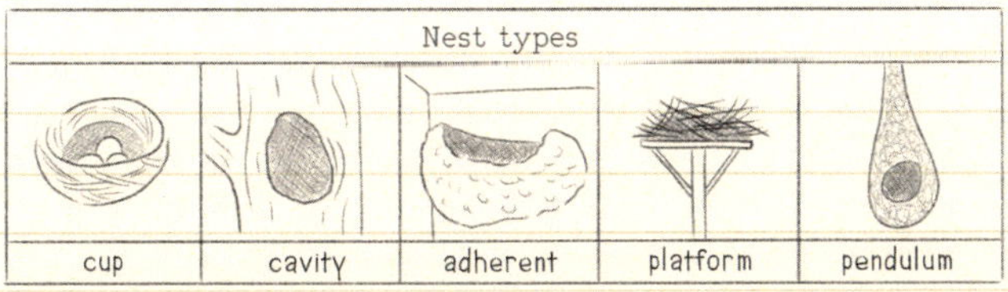

Tip: Do some research and find out what type of bird would build a nest similar to the one you've built.

29. Blueprint of Things

Although the results of this activity are similar to the Reverse Stencil one, this time we are going to get a bit more technical and let the greatest natural energy source, solar energy, imprint on photosensitive paper in a process that is similar to the one used when making photographs. Let your imagination run wild and experiment with what's near you.

Messiness Time Effort Theme

Instructions:

1. Take a piece of cyanotype paper and place it on a piece of cardboard. Make sure you are not in direct sunlight while doing this step.

2. Arrange flat natural objects onto the paper. You can use a piece of acrylic sheet or small rocks to hold everything in place.

3. Leave your paper in direct sunlight until the paper turns pale (this might take anywhere between 2 to 4 minutes, depending on how intense the sunlight is).

4. Meanwhile, prepare a container and fill it with water. Your piece of paper needs to be able to fit inside the container.

5. Bring your paper back to shade and remove everything from the the paper.

6. Immerse the paper in water for about a minute then leave to dry. Done!

Develops: The ability to follow instructions, patience, resourcefulness, intellectual curiosity and problem-solving skills.

Other ideas: Glue your finished design on the outside of a glass jar and put inside some battery-operated tealights to create a 'nature nightlight lamp'.

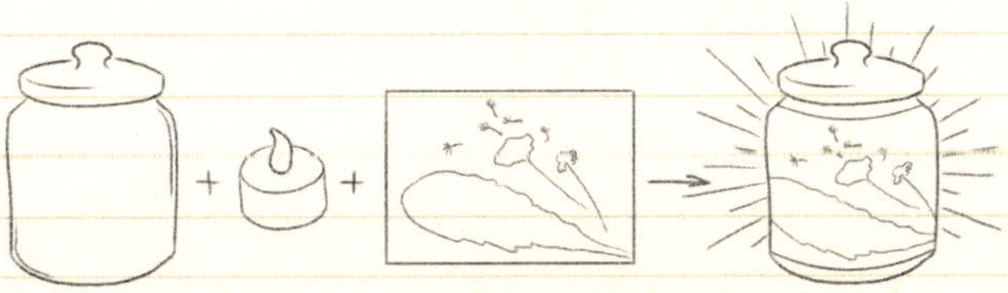

Fun fact: The word 'photography' comes from Greek and means 'drawing with light'.

Tip: Flat objects work best because they do not cast shadows whilst on the paper.

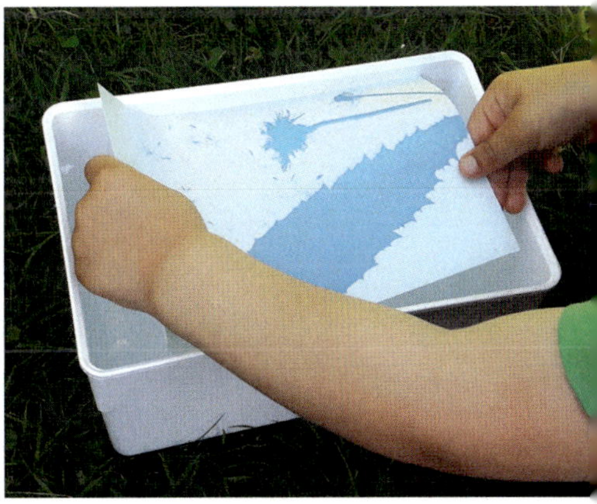

30. Looking for the Sun

The sundial is a device that shows the time by casting a shadow onto a surface. This was one of the first tools that humans used to express the passing of time. This sundial we are making will look slightly different depending on the time zone you live in – also do not expect the hours to be scattered evenly around the circle. As opposed to a proper sundial, the display will not be accurate through the year and needs to be readjusted from time to time because of increasing/decreasing daylight.

Instructions:

1. Place your sundial in a spot where you'll have sun throughout the day, with no shadows of objects (E.g. fences, trees, etc.).

2. Use a round object, about 30cm (12in) in diameter, to trace a circle on the ground.

3. Use a sharp object to make a hole in the centre of the circle and stick a straight twig inside (called a gnomon on a real sundial).

4. Craft some numbers for your sundial. You can use painted rocks, small wood slices, seashells, etc.

5. At the earliest possible hour, say 7:00 am, place an item that reads 7 on the traced circle, on the same line with the shadow.

6. Set a reminder for the next hour and repeat.

7. Do this for all the hours of the day and, at sunset, you'll have your own homemade sundial.

Develops: Understanding flow of time, patience, discipline and observational skills.

Other ideas: Use a longer stick and a wider circle if you want to log the time every 30 minutes.

Fun fact: When the Egyptians first invented sundials, they used the length of shadows to calculate the time.

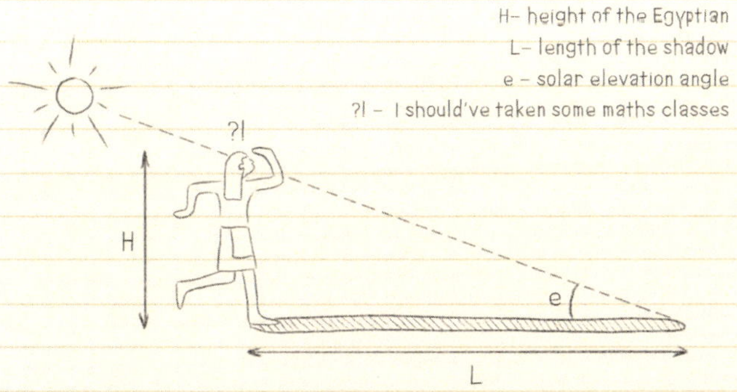

31. Nature Tray

Whenever you find yourself in nature, sharpen your observational skills – find more colourful leaves, more textured rocks, most interesting shells and funnier looking sticks. And when you get home, empty your treasure bucket, empty your pockets and place all the treasures on the table. Wait! That just looks like a pile of things! Take out the nature tray, arrange them in various ways. Now it looks like a collection of treasures, as it should.

Instructions:

1. Have fun gathering lots of treasures on your nature walks.

2. Use the tray to sort them by colour, texture, puffiness, prickliness, size, form or why not the ones that you like most?

3. Use nature books to identify them and find out their names or make the kids laugh with your made-up silly names.

4. Make sure you know what might be dangerous. If you are no mushroom expert, for example, it is safer to keep your distance.

5. Take photos with all the collected treasures and document them in a journal to check at a later time.

Develops: Curiosity, learning, exploration and the ability to focus.

Other ideas: Make your own tray. Cut a shoebox in half to make it shallow, measure it and make compartments inside. Display your findings and keep them dust-free by cutting a window on the lid and glue a transparent sheet on the inside.

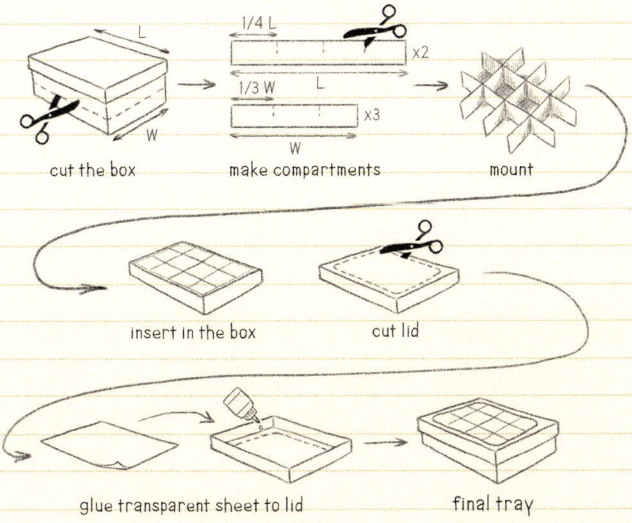

32. Leaf Flashcards

As I hope I have proven so far, there are plenty of activities that can be carried out with the pressed plants... and here is the last one in this book. This activity is about making cards by tracing the shape of a leaf. Use the cards for an association game, a leaf recognition game or a memo or domino game. You can even use the cards combined with the 'Nature Tray'.

Instructions:

1. Gather different types of leaves and press them.

2. Cut pieces of card and trace the leaves on the card with a marker.

3. Research and write down their names on the card.

4. Use contact paper or laminating sheets to cover the leaves and cut them in the same size as the cards. Make sure your leaf fits perfectly on top of the traced version.

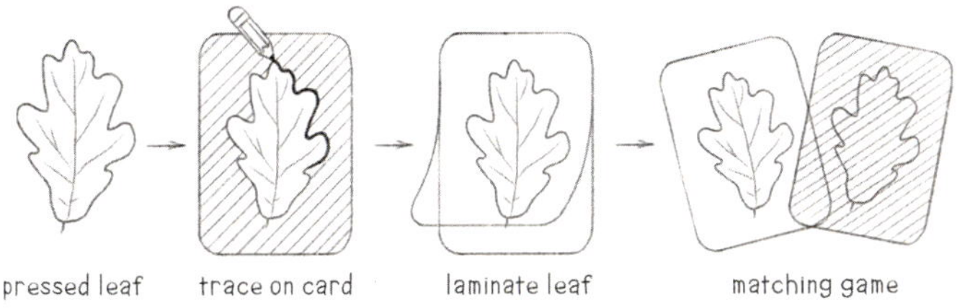

5. Play a leaf matching game while learning their names at the same time.

Develops: Concentration, cognitive development, sorting skills and creativity.

Other ideas: Laminate the leaf directly on the named card and go outside for a treasure hunt.

Tip: An iron instead of a laminator works just fine. Just use a piece of fabric on top of the laminating sheets.

33. Butterfly Life Cycle

What I'm suggesting below is a make-believe/explanatory game that goes through the butterfly life cycle. I've done it before actually raising real caterpillars until they emerged into butterflies to see if the children would find interest in the subject. The activity itself, even without the actual experience, has the potential of both teaching about the butterfly life cycle and proving all those sticks and leaves can be used in even more creative ways.

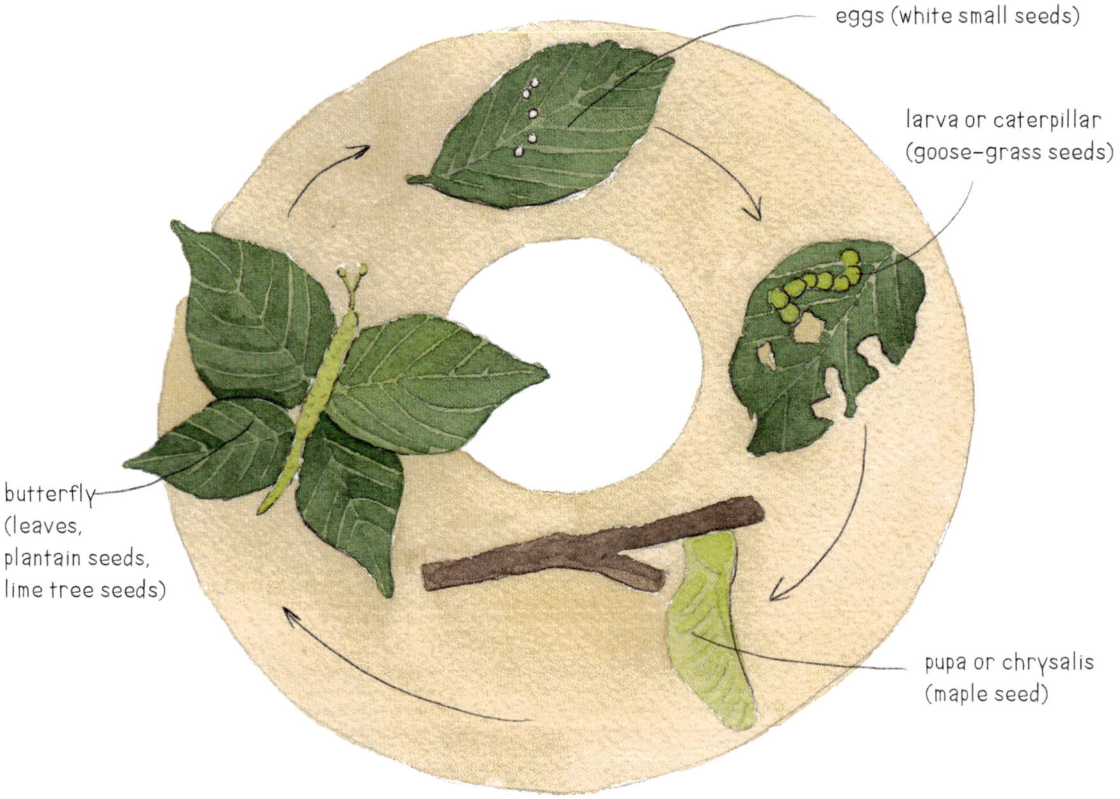

Instructions:

1. Gather nature bits and lay them out on the table.

2. Explain the process of metamorphosis using videos and storybooks to assist you.

3. Try to recreate all stages of the butterfly life cycle using the gathered material.

4. Use a marker to draw arrows between the stages to indicate the continuity of the process.

Develops: Knowledge and outside-the-box thinking.

Other ideas: Raise your own butterflies.

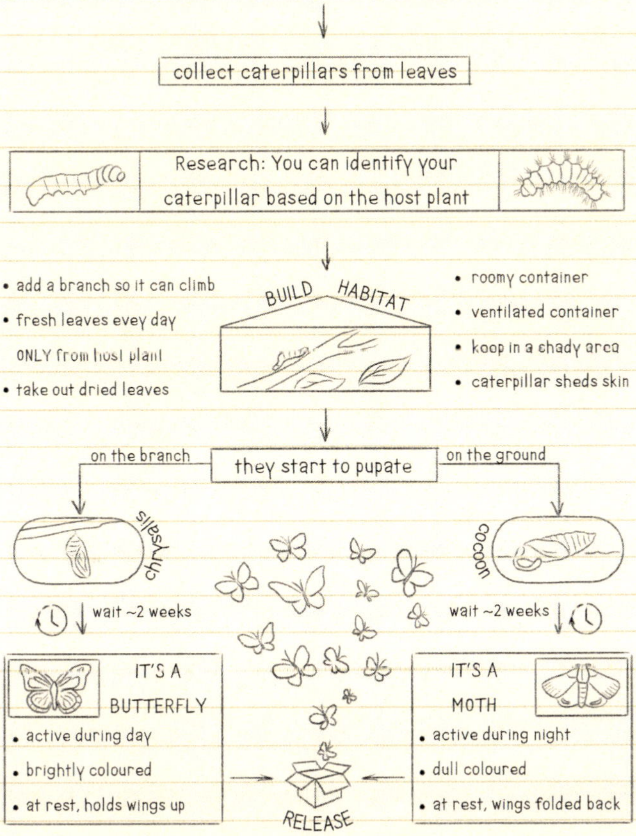

Congratulations!

Reaching this point means successful completion of all the activities in the book and maybe some of the extra ideas too. This is a great achievement for you and your little ones as well as for me as an author. It makes me feel so proud and gives me confidence that it was worth the effort I've invested in this book! I don't see this as an end. I see it more as a beginning. I'm sure you, and your little explorers, will continue the fun you have had outside, regardless of the season or the weather. Hopefully, you've enjoyed going through the activities and you had tons of fun along the way.

If you've also been keeping a journal with help from the companion workbook 'Tiny Explorers: Into the Wild – Build your own nature journal', it means you already have it all documented and the experiences are something that you'll gladly remember and can look back at. Don't forget to talk about these activities and memories long after you've completed this book. I encourage you to go back through either the journal or the photos after a while and have conversations about them. I do hope you have enjoyed the book and have created not just wonderful memories with your tiny explorers, but also a very special bond too.

Share the love for nature! Once you finish an activity or a journal page, take a photo. When you upload it on social media, tag it with #TinyExplorersIntoTheWild #TinyNookPlayground to inspire and motivate others. Check the hashtags regularly for inspiration and new ideas.

Enjoy the time spent outside!

With Love,
Miro and the Tiny Explorers

Check out tinynookplayground.com and fb.com/tinynookplayground for free printables, other activities and updates on upcoming projects.

More from the author:

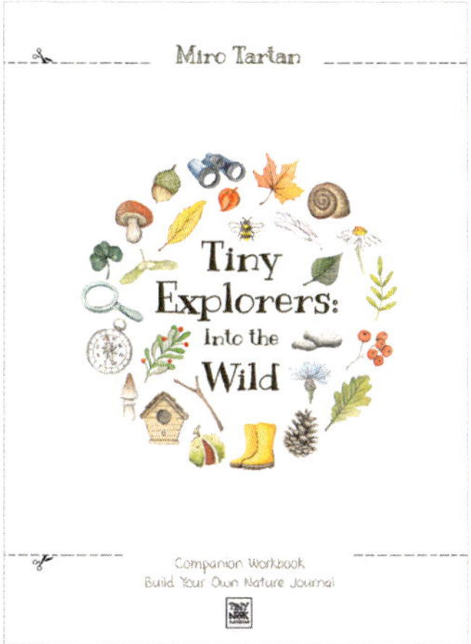

Coming soon: